Lucretius and the Modern World

Lucretius
and the
Modern World

W.R. Johnson

Duckworth

This impression 2006
First published in 2000 by
Gerald Duckworth & Co. Ltd.
90-93 Cowcross Street, London EC1M 6BF
Tel: 020 7490 7300
Fax: 020 7490 0080
inquiries@duckworth-publishers.co.uk
www.ducknet.co.uk

Quotations from R.E. Latham (tr.) *On the Nature of
the Universe by Lucretius*
(Penguin Classics, 1951) © R.E. Lathan, 1951,
reproduced by permission of Penguin Books Ltd.

A catalogue record for this book is available
from the British Library

ISBN 0 7156 2882 8
EAN 9780715628829

Typeset by Ray Davies

Contents

for Louis, again

A word of reality ... materialism first and last imbuing.
Hurrah for positive science! Long live exact demonstration!

Walt Whitman

Preface

Lucretius' poem, *On the Nature of Things*, stands as a powerful representation of classical antiquity's best and most influential effort to speculate on the material universe and the place and condition of human beings in it. Taking the atomic theory of Democritus as reformulated by Epicurus, Lucretius designed for his fellow Romans, half a century before the birth of Christ, a poetic model of the physical world they lived in and an ethical worldview that was compatible with that world, one which stressed how human beings could find ways of reducing their suffering and could then become virtuous by learning to increase their enjoyment of ordinary pleasures. This poem has been variously received since it came out of hiding at the end of the Middle Ages – it has been blamed and praised, ignored and adored. What its future can be no one can guess, but what it has meant in the past and what meanings it now offers are questions worth considering.

In the first part of this book, I provide a sketch of what I take to be the poem's central concepts and attempt to describe its ethical project and the values it espouses. In the second part, I examine several representative texts from the centuries just preceding ours, ones which reveal the ways Lucretius was read when the West was becoming modern. Here, I am especially interested in tracing the pattern of reception that created the all too familiar melancholy Lucretius and in describing how contemporary versions of 'doing' science contrast with the Lucretian version.

My notes are minimalist. A surname followed by page numbers (or, in a few cases, by a year and page numbers) indicates where the reader can go to find a more extensive discussion of the topic in question, or an opposing view, or a source for a given statement.

My quotations of Lucretius are from the Penguin translation by R.E. Latham as revised by John Godwin, and I am grateful to Penguin

Preface

Books for permission to reproduce them. There are several other good translations of the poem now available, among them Sir Ronald Melville's and W.H.D. Rouse's Loeb translation as revised by M.F. Smith. But in addition to its accuracy and clarity, Godwin's revised Penguin translation is also reader-friendly by virtue of the excellence of its introduction, its notes, its appendices, and its clear indication of how its English text accords with the line-numbering of its Latin original.

My thanks go to Susanna Morton Braund and Paul Cartledge for their very helpful suggestions for revisions, and to Deborah Blake for her generous help at every stage of the book's production.

PART I

The Poem Itself

1

No Truth But in Atoms

... that wonderful wedding of chance and necessity, happening in trillions of places at once, at a trillion different levels.

Dennett (520)

The man behind the author behind the poem

St Jerome tells us that Lucretius was born in the year 94 BCE; that a love potion rendered him insane; that he wrote his poem in random moments of sanity; that Cicero edited (or maybe proofread) the manuscript he left behind when he committed suicide at the age of forty-four. That's all the information we have about the man behind the author who wrote *On the Nature of Things*. For most of the other important Roman poets we know a bit more about their birth and death dates, about their birthplace, about their connections with their contemporaries, about their social status. Ordinarily, such near total ignorance would spare us the trouble of dealing with the life of the poet and the links between his life and his work. But the saint had prepared a heady and expert concoction that would survive when other sources of information had vanished. He fuses together erotic difficulties, madness, suicide, a manuscript left behind, unready for publication, needing the services of a literary gentleman unsympathetic to the doctrines the poem in question espoused. That turbulent untidiness and the ambiguities it generates assure Lucretius an uncertain journey through the centuries.

A couple of early Christian writers read Lucretius to refute his blasphemies against Providence and Creation and the Soul's Immortality; Jerome, with a dazzling economy of effort, fashions a collage of old gossip into a death warrant. What that collage says between its lines is: 'It's a poem filled with noble sentiments, yes; it's written in a Latin of austere beauty, yes; but it exists in a bad text, and it is, in any

3

case, the work of a nutcase. Don't bother to read it. Read Christian works, or, if you must read pagans to help your Latin style, read those with Christian inclinations (Christians of the heart) like Vergil and Cicero. But don't read *On the Nature of Things*. It is the work of a devil.'

It's a mere fluke that this cartoon survived the near destruction of Latin literature that almost gobbled up Lucretius' poem itself. But fluke or not, its influence on the readings of the poem through the centuries has been persistent and pervasive. Lucretius seems to have gone to some trouble *not* to provide his readers with any inkling of the man behind the author behind his text. But readers tend to like that sense of the human writing (speaking) to them. Alas, Jerome's phantom admirably fulfils that need. And exorcising the saint and his zombie is hard work.

The author's reader (in the poem)

As we move through the poem (*De Rerum Natura*, hereafter known as *DRN*), its author tells us little enough about himself directly, but he inevitably reveals certain traits (of the authorial temperament which might or might not have mirrored the man who created this poetic voice for this poem); he reveals these traits in the way he behaves towards his reader, the reader of the text, who is also imagined, inside the text, as a fictional character, one marked by second-person-singular pronouns, one to whom the poet addresses himself, whose moods he intuits, whose difficulties he responds to, whose welfare is the object of his deep concern. It is this reader whose dormant rational powers he is trying to stir, whose character he is trying to transform, whose life he is trying to save.

According to Lucretius, we live in a godless universe where Atoms forever move through the Void in an endless rhythm of Creation and Destruction. This simple yet complex truth is the one message that can save us from squandering our brief lives in pursuit of or flight from the countless evil illusions that disordered imaginations have concocted for us to live our lives in (the totality of these illusions we call society, civilisation, the state). It is the one message that can rescue us from being overwhelmed both by the futility we sometimes feel to be at the core of our existence and by the obverse futility, the frenzied search for

4

remedies against nothingness. For Lucretius, without the truth of Epicurus, the world is a tissue of superstitions, anxieties, savage aggressions, insatiable appetites; it is a place filled with people inflicting pain or suffering it at the hands of others, people who are 'sick unto death', compulsively searching for cures for diseases they don't understand, looking for salvation in all the wrong places. Such people, having been cheated too often by fake remedies, may find it easy to agree with Leopardi when he observes that, 'absurd though it may seem, since all reality turns out to be nothing, there is, in the world, nothing substantial, nothing real, but illusion itself', *Zibaldone*, 99).

For Lucretius, the reality of atoms moving in the void is hardly nothingness. Nor is reason, as Leopardi elsewhere surmises (213), doomed in its battle with illusion. Shaped by the gaze of Epicurus, no longer in the service of superstition, it is reason that enables us to strip away illusions for ourselves and look where Epicurus points us, to the heart of the calm. When he sees what Epicurus has taught him to see, Lucretius cries out, at the beginning of Book 3:

> You, who out of such black darkness were the first to lift up so shining a light, revealing the hidden blessings of life .... As soon as your reasoning, sprung from that godlike mind, lifts up its voice to proclaim the nature of the universe, then terrors of the mind take flight, the rampart of the world rolls apart, and I see the march of events throughout the world of space ... At this I am seized with a divine delight and a shuddering awe that by your power nature stands thus unveiled and made manifest in every part. (3.1-2, 14-17, 28-30)

This gaze and 'the divine delight and shuddering awe' that accompany it (*quaedam divina voluptas atque horror*) cannot be ours if we cannot learn how to listen to the *DRN* and make it our own with every atom of our bodies. To make this possible for us, what the poet does is to create in and for his poem a particular fictional spacetime (he and the reader inside the poem's duration, us with him in the poem), one in which he teaches his student the great, single truth and its corollary truths by seeing to it that the student learns, at each step of the way, how to understand those truths, how to think them through, each of them, for herself. So instructed, she can then free herself from illusion

5

and begin to live her life in the light and the pleasure of truth. (This is a poem about the pleasure of truth and the truth of pleasure.)

The person to whom Lucretius addresses his message is called Memmius, who was an actual Roman aristocrat, an ordinary political animal, on the make and on the take, when Julius Caesar and Catullus were reinventing, respectively, military memoir and lyric poetry (in early 50s BCE). Though Memmius certainly needed moral salvation (don't we all?), he seems at first an unlikely choice for the role Lucretius puts him in, but as a fictional device he works well enough. Whether mentioned directly by name or evoked by second-person singular pronouns and verbs, Memmius gradually incarnates the poet's ideal student/reader/convert, and, in doing that, he comes to incarnate us and our anxieties and desires as readers of a poem meant to make us anxious and desiring. (For a good discussion of how the poet constructs the figure of Memmius, see Townend, especially 270-1.)

Early in Book 5, the poet says:

> And now, Memmius ... cast your eyes on sea, lands and sky. These three bodies so different in nature, three distinct forms, three fabrics such as you behold – all these a single day will block out. The substance and structure of the world (*moles et machina mundi*), upheld through many years, will crash. I am well aware how strange and novel in its impact on the mind is this impending demolition of heaven and earth, and how hard it is for my words to carry conviction .... (91-9)

He notices that Memmius seems unconvinced. This is not the first time his student has been sceptical or obtuse. The poet tries a pinch of irony:

> It may be that force will be given to my arguments by the event itself; that your own eyes will see those violent earthquakes in a brief space dash the whole world to fragments. From such a fate may guiding fortune steer us clear! May reason rather than the event itself convince you that the whole world can collapse with one ear-splitting crack! (104-9)

Commonsense and ambition combine with sensuality and military

6

discipline to dominate the conscious part of the mind of Memmius, this reluctant atomist, so he pooh-poohs the idea of periodic and unending apocalypse as absurd. For all that, he is haunted by fears as bad or worse than this (even when he sees his 'legions thronging the Campus Martius in the ardor of mimic warfare ... magnificently armed and fired with a common purpose', 2.40-6). Perhaps, then, says the poet drily, if his conscious and unconscious minds could unite at the moment when the truth of Epicurus burst upon them from the flash and tumult of actual universal ruin and the astounded eyewitness exploded along with the ground he stood on, perhaps then he might grasp the truth? Memmius believes only what he sees with his own eyes? If he won't do his homework, maybe that's the sight he needs to see. Lucretius perishes the thought. He prays (ironically) to a fortune that Memmius worships (and he does not) to avert that final and fatal and utterly effective lesson. Let reason accomplish the task instead. Let Memmius, at long last, listen to reason.

This funny snapshot of the teacher-student dynamic functions as a sort of au revoir. Memmius will be addressed by name only three times after this, casually, almost perfunctorily; then he disappears from the poem. It's not as though he had not been warned. Very early in Book 1 the poet had said:

> ... lay aside your care and lend undistracted ears and an attentive mind to true reason. Do not scornfully reject, before you have understood them, the gifts I have marshalled for you with zealous devotion. (50-3)

A few pages later, he again cautions him against being dismissive: 'I have taught you that things cannot be created out of nothing nor, once more, be summoned back to nothing. Perhaps you are becoming mistrustful of my words, because these atoms of mine are not visible to the eye' (265-8). And a few pages later still, his troubles with Memmius elicit from the poet both a statement of his method of producing arguments (and poetry) and an ironically affectionate admission that his project of educating Memmius is probably doomed. He has been constructing elaborate proofs (or vivid metaphors) of the vacuity in seemingly solid things. Apparently Memmius has been doing a fair amount of quibbling. Lucretius cuts short this section of his lesson:

> However many pleas you advance to prolong the argument, you must end by admitting that there is vacuity in things. There are many other proofs that I could scrape together into the pile in order to strengthen conviction; but for an acute intelligence these small clues should suffice to discover the rest for yourself. As hounds often smell out the lairs of a mountain-ranging quarry screened in thickets, when once they have got on to the right trail, so in such questions one thing will lead to another, till you can succeed by yourself in tracking down the truth to its lurking place and dragging it forth. (398-409)

For the ideal reader (not Memmius) who is being constructed out of the raw material Memmius furnishes (as we read/listen along with him), the few clues will suffice his acute intelligence, and he will be able to hunt down truth in its lair and, imitating Epicurus, drag it into the light (of his mind). That reader will learn the method of (Epicurean) thinking in the same way that the students of Socrates learn (but they mostly don't) Socratic thinking; he will learn to think by thinking through questions from one problem to another: tireless hunting dogs following the scent once they've got it till they find what they're looking for. Memmius isn't like that.

> If you grow weary and relax from the chase, there is one thing, Memmius, that I can safely promise you: my honeyed tongue will pour from the treasury of my breast such generous draughts, drawn from inexhaustible springs, that I am afraid slow plodding age may creep through my limbs and unbolt the bars of my life before the full flood of my arguments on a single point has flowed in verse through your ears. (410-17)

They are not half way through Book 1 and the poet already sees his disciple nodding off. Athletic he may be, but this is one chase he was not born for. The cascade of verifying metaphors has stupefied him. But the poet cheerfully assures him that there are plenty more where those came from. He has a sudden vision of the both of them as

8

doddering old men. He is, compulsively, still spouting metaphors from the inexhaustible cornucopia of his imagination, and Memmius, one foot in the grave, still can't be bothered to pay attention. It's a droll cartoon, this, in which Memmius is not unsweetly told he's not cut out for atomism, and in which the poet's own obsession with 'getting it right' finds a comic shape. Making these metaphors for the truth is Lucretius' reason for being. He speaks of it elsewhere (e.g. 2.730, 3.419) as a sweet labour. It keeps him up all night (1.142-5), and even when he's sleeping, while lawyers dream of law courts and generals dream of leading their troops and sailors of outwitting the wind and the sea, the poet dreams: 'I go on with my task, for ever exploring the nature of the universe and setting down my discoveries in my native tongue' (4.966-70).

Near the opening of Book 1 (140-2), after emphasising the difficulty of the task of finding Latin equivalents for Greek ideas and words, Lucretius had told Memmius: 'the joy I hope to derive from our delightful friendship' (*sperata voluptas suavis amicitiae* – big Epicurean words, Pleasure and Friendship) 'encourages me to face the task however hard.' Yet for all Lucretius' dedication and resolve, his dialogue with Memmius is not successful in the poem, and this failure the Beckettian picture of the incompatible old men neatly emphasises. Memmius is, at one level, a symbol of the difficulty of being instructed, and his failures remind us that listening is a difficult art (think here of Socrates and his Alcibiades, of Aristotle and his Alexander, of Seneca and his Nero) and that students sometimes mishear or do not hear at all. That function is crucial for the poem, but more crucial still is the function that remains after the name and the figure of Memmius have faded away.

The fiction of Memmius creates the right situation of discourse for Lucretius' message, one in which the poet can inform and argue with and comfort his ideal/actual reader, as the need arises:

Desist, therefore, from thrusting our reasoning from your mind because of its disconcerting novelty. Weigh it, rather, with discerning judgment. Then, if it seems true to you, give in. If it is false, gird yourself to oppose it. For the mind wants to discover by reasoning what exists in the infinity of space that lies out there, beyond the ramparts of the world – that region into which the intellect longs to peer and into which the free projection of the mind does actually extend its flight. (2.1040-7).

By this moment in the poem, the reader knows she will eventually, if she sticks to it, become the poet's sparring partner, his equal, his accomplice. There are some wonderful splotches of local colour in the poem (pictures of Italy and its countryside, glimpses of Rome and its noise and dirt and glitter), but the poem derives most of its most powerful illusion of immediacy from the intensity of the dialogic spacetime its teacher and student share: what we believe in, what we hear and focus on, is what the teacher is saying to the student, how he tries to anticipate, not least by the wealth of his verifying metaphors, the uncertainties and the doubts of his student. We watch Socrates 'teach' his students in the midst of a brilliantly realised Athens. In Lucretius (the rhetorical/poetic intimacy is, for different reasons, as effective here as it is in St Augustine's equally didactic *Confessions*), we become the student in a poem that is both in Rome and not anywhere specific. What matters is the teaching voice and our answers and questions to it.

The lazy, casually sceptical reader in the text whom Memmius impersonates gradually gives way to a more responsible reader in the text (us, you and I), and that allows the irritable (fanatical? tyranni-cal?) performer of the poem to yield space and time to someone more even-tempered and less likely to snap at Memmius-Us. The fact remains, however, that the voice of the poem, the sum of all the speaker's teacherly moods and stratagems, is always on or near the boil, he seldom shows the suavity and steady-cool that are uniformly evident in the manner of the speaker of Brian Greene's *The Elegant Universe*. In that exemplary prose-poem on string theory and the marriage of general relativity and quantum mechanics, the leisurely flow of verifying metaphors moves steadily, placidly (Imagine this, Imagine that, Now Imagine this: these words resemble Lucretius', but their music is less edgy). In Greene, the fecundity of metaphor is matched by a superb equanimity. Lucretius is not (as I hope to con-vince you) melancholy, but, although equanimity (*ataraxia*) is the supreme Epicurean virtue, Lucretius is, for the purposes of his poem at any rate, never quite poised, always the satiric preacher, ready to tumble, when need be, from the merely ironic to the sardonic. He is on (the) edge, and wants us to be there.

Gods and monsters and Epicurus

Why does he want, so much, to convince us (us, not Memmius – he knows that Memmius is a lost cause), why does he need to save us from ourselves? He never tells us why, never tells us the story of how he himself was saved or who it was saved *him*. Maybe one day at a bookstall he chanced to pick up a copy of Epicurus' *On Nature* (Sedley 71-2, 91-2, 144), read a few sentences, read a few more, decided to buy the book; took it home, read a bit more; stayed up all night reading it; read it again; never stopped reading it. Such things happen.

In any case, however it happened, he was 'reborn' (and is now himself a midwife):

O joyless hearts of men! O minds without vision! How dark and dangerous the life in which this tiny span is lived away! Do you not see that nature is barking for two things only, a body free from pain, a mind released from worry and fear for the enjoyment of pleasurable sensations? (2.14-19)

Like a watchdog (or a satirist, one descended from the dogs of the Cynic, Diogenes), Nature herself repeats her warning barks whose jist is: 'Flee pain and the near occasions of pain! Seek real pleasures by getting rid of the bad mental habits that ruin our delight in the goodness of being alive.' Other purveyors of other salvations warn the wicked and the weak against sins that will corrupt them and so require their being cast into outer darkness. For Lucretius, sins are the symptoms, not the cause, of our wretchedness. There seems to be darkness around us, to be sure, but it is not real darkness, it is the darkness of our ignorance, of our misimaginings. We are not things that came from nothing and that go to nothing (that is what we fear); instead, we, like all things else, are made of atoms in the void, or rather, we are made of atoms *and* the vacuity in which the atoms move. We exist, not in darkness, but in a pinpoint of light between what seems the nothingness from which we came and what seems the nothingness into which we are going (but the atoms that compose us

11

are eternal: they are not nothing or nothingness). That sliver of time (*hoc aevi quodcumque* = this whatever-it-turns-out-to-be-of-time) we waste or spoil, doubling its darkness with crazy notions of divine wrath and divine punishment, with stupid efforts to hide from our fears and our disappointments or to abolish them or be distracted from them with power and money or other futile stratagems that generate perpetual discord in our societies. If we can learn to imagine things as they are, atoms in their void, endlessly dispersing and reconfiguring, our guilts, our fears, our false desires for unreal cures and unreal pleasures, our *illusions*, will disappear. Having learned to rid ourselves of our mental pains, we'll be more likely to deal adequately with most physical pain. Finally, we will then be free to enjoy ourselves, to see accurately and to delight (briefly perhaps but richly) in the ephemeral configurations of atoms that we call ourselves and the world. 'Altogether, at each moment, and in every particular, we are in the hands of some alien, inscrutable power.' That is Santayana's description of a primordial religious emotion. Replace his singular with 'powers', and you have a fair sketch of Roman religion (Sir Frank Adcock once opined that if the ancient Romans had ridden bicycles, they would have had a goddess named Punctura). The world is filled with danger (fire, flood, thunder, heat and cold, ravenous beasts, merciless barbarians). Some of these perils we can sometimes cope with, but mostly we are 'strangers and afraid in a world we never made'. We need to get control of these hostile forces, but we are powerless to do so. Therefore, we develop a technology of supplication and appeasement. Our fear and our guilt we project onto unseen masters. Our superegos, in short, become divine. They begin to control the powers that threaten us. Sometimes they don't do what we ask of them, but more often than not they seem to help us out. When they fail us too often, we get new gods. DO UT DES. I give (you a sacrifice) in order that you may give (me what I'm asking for). When you stop giving, I stop giving.

That cluster of beliefs constituted a somewhat naive yet eminently rational effort to control the gods who control the universe. Naturally, one was not able to believe in this style of religious technology constantly or completely. It did fail from time to time, and even when it worked, one got the sense that one's version of it was, to put it kindly, inadequate. At such times, horrendous prodigies appeared with scary regularity (in Livy's wonderful history of Rome, they enter and exit like clockwork, deliciously). One's dreams turned ghastly. There were, it seemed, monstrous things down there, out there (X-Files, anyone?). The gods and the monsters now seemed cut from the same cloth. We feel guilty because of bad things we've done, and the powers we've created will punish us for them in this life or (and) in another, later one. We feel angry at the powers we created for their impotence. (This anger is, of course, especially keen when the inadequacy of one's *tribal* gods is revealed by their defeat on a battlefield; at such moments we cannot ignore the possibility that our tribal gods, and gods in general, are essentially political entities.) We feel frightened because neither we nor the powers we created can protect us from the world or from ourselves. Our superegos are having a nervous breakdown.

That's when Epicurus steps into the picture:

When human life lay grovelling in all men's sight, crushed to the earth under the dead weight of superstition (*gravi sub religione*) whose grim features loured menacingly upon mortals from the four quarters of the sky, a man from Greece was first to raise mortal eyes in defiance, first to stand erect and brave the challenge. Fables of gods did not crush him, nor the lightning flash and the growling menace of the sky. Rather, they quickened the keen courage of his heart, so that he, first of all men, longed to smash the constraining locks of nature's doors. The vital vigour of his mind prevailed. He ventured far out beyond the flaming ramparts of the world and voyaged in mind throughout infinity. Returning victorious, he proclaimed to us what can be and what cannot, how the power of each thing is limited, and its boundary stone sticks buried deep. Therefore superstition in its turn lies crushed beneath his feet, and we by his triumphs are lifted level with the skies. (1.62-79)

Fama deum nec fulmina. Epicurus was intimidated neither by 'the fame of the gods nor by the thunderbolts' that myths about the gods bestow on them. It was not gods that his defabricating strategies were aimed at. He was an extremely pious person, very concerned to describe the nature of the gods and to suggest how we might best go about revering them. But he had no patience with traditional religious discourses that anthropomorphise divinities and inflict on them the responsiblity for controlling reality. In a passage marked by a chilling, sinister lyricism, the murder of Iphigenia by her father, King Agamemnon, reveals how politicians use 'beautiful' holy lies to camouflage ugly means and ends: 'Raised by the hands of men, she was brought trembling to the altar. Not for her the sacrament of marriage and the loud chant of Hymen. It was her fate in the very hour of marriage to fall a sinless victim to a sinful rite, slaughtered to her greater grief by a father's hand, so that a fleet might sail under happy auspices. Such are the heights of wickness to which men have been driven by superstition' (or 'religious awe'), 95-101. *Tantum religio potuit suadere malorum*: here, culminating in what is probably the poem's most famous line, the girl's slaughter represents every good thing (whatever is useful or beautiful, whatever gives or gets pleasure) that perverted desire destroys to achieve its goals when, trying to guard itself or medicate itself, it attempts to secure what is neither natural nor necessary, what it doesn't truly need, what will eventually cause it, and probably others, lots of pain.

From the Christian perspective, the poet of the *DRN* is essentially an atheist because he utterly denies Creation and Providence and the Soul's Immortality, along with other essential features of the Christian cosmic comfort system. He does, however, believe in gods, and, in his own way, his piety towards them is admirable in its purity. Contemplating the universe revealed by the gaze of Epicurus, Lucretius sees, and causes us to see:

> The majesty of the gods ... and those quiet habitations, never shaken by storms or drenched by rain-clouds or defaced by white drifts of the snow which a harsh frost congeals. A cloudless ether roofs them and laughs with radiance lavishly diffused. All their wants are supplied, and nothing at any time cankers their peace of mind. (3.18-24)

It is this vision of divine equipoise, combined with his gaze on the dynamism of atomic movement (a superb counterpoint), that induces in the poet 'a kind of delight and shuddering awe' (see p. 4), an ecstasy that is at once intellectual and carnal (why be shy here? the picture and the tone are erotic). The iconography of the heavenly habitation is borrowed from three lines of Homer (*Odyssey* 6.43-5), but Lucretius elaborates on the original's play with light and ironises it deftly: in the Homeric passage, Athena is winging her way to Olympus. In Greek poetry, the top of the gods' mountain may be free from inclement weather, but, as Lucretius sees it, that's just myth: the real peak of the real Olympus is beset by intolerable weather. But the gods of Epicurus, they are off in another part of the galaxy. They toil not neither do they spin. They have no purpose, they are perdurable but not immortal. What they do have, because they understand things as they are, is imperturbability. Hence they are, until the moment of their their inevitable disintegration, in a state of perpetual *divina voluptas atque horror*. If they notice our planet and us at all, they don't pay us much attention. Our pleasures and pains are insignificant to them. Their perspectives are longer, wider, higher:

> Bear this well in mind, and you will immediately perceive that nature is free and uncontrolled by proud masters (*dominis superbis*) and runs the universe by herself without the aid of gods who pass their unruffled lives, their placid aeon, in calm and peace! – who can rule the sum total of the measureless? Who can hold in coercive hand the strong reins of the unfathomable? Who can spin all the firmaments alike and foment with the fires of ether all the fruitful earths? Who can be in all places at all times, ready to darken the clear sky with clouds and rock it with a thunderclap – to launch bolts that may often wreck his own temples, or retire and spend his fury letting fly at deserts with that missile which often passes by the guilty and slays the innocent and blameless? (2.1090-1104)

Traditional theology has attracted the satirist's notice. His derision of divine omnipotence and divine omnipresence may seem naive to believers whose faiths are rooted in representations of immaterial ontology. But for strict materialists these objections to traditional versions of godhead are the norm. Yet less important than illusions about the god's limitless power and presence (the god he is thinking of here, as we see from 6.387-404, is Rome's supreme tribal god, Jupiter) are his silliness and his wickedness: he destroys his own temples and he punishes the innocent haphazardly along with the guilty (for the poet, these ways are not 'mysterious' but ridiculous; admittedly, the village atheist might conceive similar objections, but the village atheist could not write the passage in Book 6, much less the *DRN* itself; and, of course, to use a contemporary instance, it does not take a village atheist to point out that, despite the repeated prayers of the Reverend Pat Robertson, hurricanes demolish Christian Suburbias no less frequently than Gay Ghettos).

If myths about the gods were merely untrue, there would be little harm in them. But these myths are in fact poisonous. On the one hand, they nourish what is worst in human passions and human unreason and provoke even decent people to do wicked things; and, on the other, they keep us from contemplating the real gods and their equipoise, which is a good way (combined with studying Epicurus) of attaining the kind of spiritual balance that human beings should fervently aspire to (but seldom or never can completely attain).

That balance is impossible even to think of, much less work toward, as long as people imagine that their fates and their daily lives (not to mention their imaginary afterlives, not to mention the safety and prosperity of their State) depend on the whims of invisible, incomprehensible Super-Beings. The mental habits that form themselves around this version of humans and their place in the universe churn hope and fear into a maelstrom of unreason. The human mind produced by this regimen is essentially paranoid, it is a short-circuited constellation of anger, resentment, despair and guilt. Perhaps guilt is the root of all evil, guilt which is displaced hatred and fear. We want to abjure the wicked and insane gods (the arrogant masters) who watch and wait for us to stumble, who promise us lemonade and give us shit, but we don't dare to do that (so we hate and fear them more and more, as our disappointments grow, and our rage and our hunger). We feel worthless, we feel doomed. The poet has a solution to this institutionalised torment. He deletes Hell from our cultural map:

> As for those torments that are said to take place in the depths of Acheron, they are actually present here and now, in our own lives. There is no wretched Tantalus, as the myth relates, transfixed with groundless terror at the huge boulder poised above him in the air. But in this life there are really mortals oppressed by unfounded fear of the gods and trembling at the impending

doom that may fall on any of them at the whim of chance. (3.979-83)

Lacking the light that Epicurus offers us, we are driven by desire for what destroys us, for bad pleasures that promise mere diversion or final salvation but that instead produce pain and destruction ('forever feeding a malcontent mind, filling it with good things but never satisfying it', 1001-3). Unprotected by atomistic truth, we are crushed by fear and by guilt: 'darkened by the fear of retribution for our misdeeds ... the conscience-ridden mind in terrified anticipation torments itself with its own goads and whips ... so at length the life of misguided mortals becomes a Hell on earth' (1014-23).

In a sense, what bothers Lucretius most here is that it is our instinct for sanity that brings about our greatest unhappiness by fabricating in our minds a kind of cruel machine for the production of exponential pain. In its moments of desire, when the mind's movement towards its 'good' begins, if it has been tainted with images of false gods, of false punishments and false rewards, it will turn away from the path that would lead it to its proper pleasure and it will head, almost automatically, for its unnecessary pain. This 'road taken' stirs the ever-ready satirist to work; he mocks at his culture's false gods and the imaginary monsters (Cerberus and the Furies, 1011) which enact their fake just wrath and fake just punishments (fake, but with real consequences in the minds of those who entertain them). Tormented by pains both real and unreal in this life and by thoughts of the unreal pains that await us in the unreal afterlife, we face our real pain stupid with exhaustion, and we further confuse ourselves in the blind pursuit of foolish or evil remedies.

'Because you are always pining for what is not,' says Nature to an old man who clings to his life, 3.957-60, 'and are unappreciative of the things at hand, your life has slipped away unfulfilled and unprized, Death has stolen upon you unawares, before you are ready to retire from life's banquet filled and satisfied.' Having failed to enjoy the beauty and goodness of this life, we compound a normal fear of death with irrational resentments against death, and even when we have managed to reject the myths of eternal punishment, we continue to mistake the dread of dying with the fear of being dead, refusing to admit that 'being dead' is a wild oxymoron, a perfect example of

17

'contradiction in terms'. These obstacles to enlightenment endure some of the poet's funniest, bitterest pages at the end of Book 3 (870ff.). In passing, we should not ignore some witty verses in which the satirist has some fun with mystic notions of pre-natal being and of reincarnation. He imagines the eager returnees (Shirley MacLaine among them?) as voyeurs at the parental bed:

> It is surely ludicrous to suppose that spirits are standing by at the mating and birth of animals – a numberless number of immortals on the look-out for mortal frames, jostling and squab-bling to get in first and establish themselves firmly. Or is there perhaps an established compact that first come shall be first served, without any trial of strength between spirit and spirit? (3.776-83)

Where and who were we before we came here, where and who will we be when we're gone? These questions obsess us because we hate the truth that we guess at and cannot bear (Stove, 119, 128). The poet has Death ask us:

> Will *you* kick and protest against your sentence? ... You, who waste the major part of you time asleep and, when you are awake, are snoring still and dreaming. You, who bear a mind hag-ridden by baseless fear and cannot find the commonest cause of your distress, hounded as you are, pathetic creature, by a pack of troubles and drifting in a drunken stupor upon a wavering tide of fantasy. (3.1045-52)

The truth of the atoms, speaking in the voice of Nature, reminds us of the reality that we (of whom the old man is the extreme cartoon) refuse to regard: 'The old is always thrust aside to make way for the new, and one thing must be built out of the wreck of others ... There is need of matter, so that later generations may arise; when they have lived out their time, they will all follow you' (964-5, 967-8). This, as we will presently see, is a great, perhaps the greatest, the central, theme of the poem. It is the wisdom of Empedocles (Sedley, 21ff., 201f.) fused with the wisdom of Epicurus, Love and Strife seen under the sign of the atoms. 'Bygone generations have taken your road,' continues

18

Nature, 'and those to come will take it no less. So one thing will never cease to spring from another. To none is life given in freehold; to all on lease' (969-71). Between one seeming darkness and another is this (our) patch of brightness which we can understand and cherish only when we see and acknowledge and bless its amazing (plentiful) brevity: 'Look back at the eternity that passed before we were born, and mark how utterly it counts to us as nothing. This is a mirror that Nature holds up to us, in which we may see the time that shall be after we are dead. Is there anything terrifying in the sight – anything depressing – anything that is not more restful than the soundest sleep?' (972-7).

Well, yes, now that you mention it, there is indeed something terrifying and depressing here, something grim enough to ruin anyone's beauty sleep. Trapped in sheer illusion, beset by pains both real and unreal, between one nothingness and another, why should we not feel – uneasy? As we will see in Chapter 4, many readers of the poem have been unwilling to take the poet at his word here, they have suspected that he himself sleeps much less well than he claims, that he looks in Nature's mirror and feels more horror than Pascal ever dreamt of when contemplating heaven's immensities. Later, I will be arguing that the poet does practice what he preaches, that he looks at the past and the future, rejoices in his small/vast present, and sleeps the sleep of the happy atomist. But he wants us to admit here, and elsewhere, that we are terrified – by what our vanishing ignorance teaches us, as we glimpse, behind the illusions we were born into, the beginnings of atomistic truth. That terror is the opposite of the divine delight and shuddering awe that take hold of him when he sees the atoms cascading, at the speed of light, through the universe of Epicurus. Admitting that terror is, for the poet, the beginning of wisdom. It is what he tries to get us to admit to throughout the poem (and, spectacularly, at its close). Only when we have torn ourselves free from supernatural terrors and placebos, can the work of reformation begin.

And when we have really begun to kick the habit of false pain and its false analgesics, we can begin to look at the real gods, those emblems of real pleasure. At the opening of Book 6, before he begins to explain the sky and its phenomena, he remarks that people are frightened by what happens in the heavens because they imagine that it is angry gods that let loose thunder and violent winds and rain.

> It may happen that men who have learnt the truth about the carefree existence of the gods fall to wondering by what power the universe is kept going, especially those movements that are seen overhead in the ethereal borderland. Then the poor creatures are plunged back into their old superstitions and saddle themselves with cruel masters whom they believe to be all-powerful. (6.58-64)

Those who had set their feet upon the ladder have slipped, have suffered a relapse. They had not completely understood that the gods are carefree, they had forgotten what atomic movement means. Meteorological disasters had shaken them out of their wits and had erased what they learned. Blind reasoning has slipped back into its old groove and has misled them – back into their old errors and terrors.

> Unless you vomit such notions out of your mind and banish far away all thoughts unworthy of the gods and foreign to their tranquillity, then the holy beings whom you thus diminish will often do you real harm. This is not because the supreme majesty of the gods can in fact be wronged so as to be tempted in a fit of anger to wreak a savage revenge. No, the fault will be in you. Because you will picture the quiet ones in their untroubled peace as tossed on turbulent waves of anger, you will not approach their temples with a tranquil heart; you will not be able to admit into a breast at peace those images emanating from a holy body that bring to the minds of men their tidings of a form divine. From this you can gather what sort of life must ensue. (6.68-79)

respuis means 'spit out' rather than 'vomit', but the latter mirrors the violence of the poet's warning. Remembering that its foul taste signals poison, you must immediately expel what you have ingested unawares. Entering the gods' temples with a heart that the truth of atomism has begun to cleanse, the convert (we might as well call her that) gazes on the divine images of perfect equipoise, and those images, passing through her eyes into her mind and heart, help and hasten the work of its cleansing. But seekers whose knowledge of atomism has been weakened or destroyed will return to the temples for the wrong reasons. Like runaway slaves, they will creep back in fear and trembling, they will pray and make vows, as if the gods could or would banish what they fear or confer what they desire. Addicted once again to their passions and to the delusions those passions beget, their ids and superegos morph back and forth as their sins and guilts wax and wane. Back again in the old life, their sufferings increase because, remembering their brief freedom, they find their old delusions are magnified by 'bad faith'.

The corruption of the best is the worst. Just before this definitive passage on the equipoise of the gods, its meaning for humans, and the dangers of relapse, the poet had begun Book 6 with his final tribute to the human being who had brought salvation to human kind. Like Hercules (see 5.23-54) and the heirs of Alexander, the divine kings of Egypt, Epicurus is also a *sôtêr*, a saviour, but he surpasses these cultural and political heroes, both mythical and historical, because, seeing the human condition as it actually is, he devised real remedies for what really harms human lives:

> He saw that, practically speaking, all that was wanted to meet men's vital needs was already at their disposal, and, so far as could be managed, their livelihood was assured. He saw some men in the full enjoyment of riches and reputation, dignity and authority, and happy in the fair fame of their children. Yet for all that, he found aching hearts in every home, racked incessantly by pangs the mind was powerless to assuage, forced to vent themselves in recalcitrant repining. (6.9-16)

How is it possible that reason and energy and good fortune could unite and produce misery – everywhere? Why is it that those who achieve what they desire, and retain what they gain, are as miserable as those who fail of their desires? There are bad things in the world and its contingencies (bad things happening everywhere, all the time), but as bad or worse than those evils are the ones the mind makes by itself for itself. The mind is powerless to assuage those evils because it is the mind that devises them. So, the fault is with the mind and with the will whose partner is the mind.

21

He concluded that the source of this illness was the container itself, which infected with its own malady everything that was collected from outside and brought into it, however beneficial. He arrived at this conclusion partly because he perceived that the container was cracked and leaky, so that it could never by any possibility be filled; partly because he saw it tainted whatever it took in with the taste of its own foulness. (16-23)

Lucretius had used this image back when he was describing how real evils/pains in the world become punishments in the afterlife of Myth and of Religion (he is talking of the Danaids, condemned forever to fetch water in sieves for having murdered their husbands at their father's command):

To be forever feeding a malcontent mind, filling it with good things but never satisfying it – the fate we suffer when the circling seasons enrich us with their products and ever-changing charms although we are never filled with the fruits of life – this surely exemplifies the story of those maidens in the flower of life forever pouring water into a leaking vessel that can never by any technique be filled. (3.1003-10)

As we will see in the next chapter, it is the triumphant (yet disastrous) partnership between humanity's limitless desire and its fecund inge-nuity that shapes Lucretius' version of morality. Lacking the light of Epicurus, this partnership promotes and in a sense ensures our real misery. We cannot get enough, we seem unable to find ways of getting enough, and more than enough and more than that. The fruits of life, plentifully supplied by the seasons' changes, give us enough of what is both natural and necessary, but that abundance doesn't satisfy our insatiable desire for illusions, a desire which irrational reason eggs on and abets. The Danaids had all they needed (husbands: that's the sexist myth), but they destroyed, in their folly, their share of good, and now they enact compulsively the despair of trying to secure what is lost and cannot be regained. Their sieves are like their minds, their minds are like ours.

Our desires are naturally limitless, like the vessels that attempt to hold them: our minds, our imaginations, our wills, our memories, wherein desire and fear effect their representations of who we are and what we want. The only way of placing a check upon this system of desire is to learn the difference between desires that are natural but not necessary (regular hot baths instead of an occasional cold one, more food and sleep than our bodies require) and needs that are necessary (some sleep, some food, evacuation, adequate seasonal garments); then, having learned that, to learn the difference between needs or desires that are natural or necessary or both and cravings or whims or obsessions that are neither necessary nor natural (make your own list of these; making these three lists is a tricky, interesting exercise; maybe it tells us something about our culture, our values and our self). But trimming back desires (not trying to eradicate them, which is the puritan's remedy) is only half the problem. Our desires are nourished by our brains, which have a tendency to misrepresent to us our sensations, to convert what we see and hear into harmful misperceptions, into visions of gods and monsters which threaten us, to transform these phantoms into 'reasons'. For desires to be trimmed, our minds must be cleansed.

Good reason and good desire work to make our brief existence here a possible spacetime in which we can discover and enjoy good and real and true pleasure (that is the Gospel of True Pleasure; yes, this is a religion, one with its own form – materialist – of cosmic comfort). Bad reason and bad desire unite to create an indefatigable search for pleasures that promise relief from various dangers and pains but that instead increase real dangers and exacerbate real pain. What to do? First call in a tinker to repair the vessel. Then scour it again and again till it glistens, till all trace of the taint has vanished. Now the mind is capable of accurately representing what the self sees and hears, now the will desires what it needs, now the task of learning the truths of atomism can begin again, and the gospel of true pleasure can fill the vessel to its brim. Seeing the leaky, filthy vessel, Epicurus

> purged men's breasts with words of truth. He set bounds to desire and fear. He demonstrated what is the highest good, after which we all strive, and pointed the way by which we cannot achieve it, keeping straight ahead on a narrow track. (6.24-8)

The highest good is not, as some maintain, facing the grimmest truth

23

(Clay) or unlearning the fear of death (Segal) or otherwise achieving the absence of pain; the highest good is true pleasure, that is to say, a process (not a thing or a condition) in which the human being works to keep pain as far away from himself as possible and uses that relative absence of pain to enjoy the 'miracle' of beauty, utility, plenitude, and delight that results (for the human mind) from the vision of the contingencies of the atoms in their void, from the fact that our world has come into existence 'through the spontaneous and casual collision and the multifarious, accidental, random and purposeless congregation and coalescence of atoms whose suddenly formed combinations could serve on each occasion as the starting-point of substantial fabrics – earth and sea and sky and the races of living creatures' (2.1058-63; for a contemporary version, 'The essence of life is statistical improbability on a colossal scale,' see Dawkins 317 and *passim*; Dennett 180-1, 519-20 and *passim*). It is with his revelation of this amazing, incredible, breathtaking, stupendous chance clustering of matter ('which the ether clasps in ardent embrace', Love and Strife, 1066), that Epicurus purifies our minds and our desires and teaches us his divine (godlike) and divinely moral hedonism.

Nature's and the poem's design

Dalzell (1982, 217), having noted that the poem seems to have escaped its final revision, proceeds to offer this elegant description of its structure:

> As it stands, the poem has a rational and satisfying structure. It is divided into three parts, each consisting of two books. The first and third parts deal with physical doctrine, the microcosm of the atom in Books 1 and 2 and the macrocosm of the universe in Books 5 and 6. Between these two outer panels the central section describes the Epicurean doctrine of the soul, the senses, the mind and the will. Each of the six books begins with a formal prologue and ends with an extended passage of particular interest or striking poetry. The first book in each pair is more systematic in argument, the second is generally more relaxed and discursive.

24

That lucid shape vividly manifests itself when one closes the volume and backs off from the poem, but while one is actually involved in the pleasures of the text, one's experiences are more varied and sometimes contradictory. If one often has 'an impression of logical exactness' that 'sweeps the reader on with an imposing array of balanced proofs', one also feels from time to time that 'this impression of systematic progression is misleading: for if we attempt to follow the argument closely, we soon discover a number of passages where the logical connexion is elusive'. Dalzell is unwilling to blame all these 'inadequacies on the textual tradition or the incompleteness of the poem'; but, in any case, in spite of them, 'the general impression which the work creates is of great structural simplicity and strength'. How to account for this (accurate) description of something like a formal antinomy (its unity, its dispersions) in the poem's texture?

The architecture of the poem and the linear motion through time (and argument) that it prescribes are indeed possessed of all the clarity and power that Dalzell discovers in them. The openings and closings of books, the pairing and contrasting of books, the parts and their sum, their parallels and countervailings, like a Roman bridge, a Roman aqueduct, a Roman road, seem incarnations of simplicity and of severe strength. But that perspective on the poem does not take into account other structural features that throw the poem's architectonics into superb relief, that enhance its spatial perfections by counterpointing them.

One of these we have already examined, the dialogue of teacher/reader. Not a few of the logical wobblings that Dalzell points to occur when the teacher is forcing his reader to negotiate her way through a special maze of arguments in order for her to glimpse a particular truth in its full clarity (Jenkyns 236, 275). I'm hardly claiming that Lucretius never erred in presenting his argument (or that the text of the passage in question is always accurate or fully revised). But I do feel that inside the majestic and massive space of the poem, inside the *time* of the dialogue, while performing the poem along with its poet-teacher, we are enjoying something different from aesthetic awe at its construction (Dalzell 1998, 56). Engaged in a sort of dialogic rough-and-tumble, we are having mostly serious fun as we are put through our paces, for at the same time we are listening to a satirist of genius make bitter fun of his country's religion and politics, of his philosophical opponents living and dead. And, of course, of his reader, you, me:

> If you cannot account for what you see happen without inventing particles of matter with the same sort of nature as the whole objects [they configure] ... you will have to postulate particles that shake their sides with uproarious guffaws and bedew their cheeks with salt tears. (1.915-20)

The poet likes this joke about chortling atoms so much that he repeats it (2.976-86). This dimension of the poem, its frequent, satiric disruptions, shape an impression that contravenes the impression of 'classical', 'simplicity and strength' and of sustained philosophic argument that Dalzell rightly identifies in the poem. The opposing impression is of something jagged and raucous: we can't settle back, relax and listen. We can't quite find our footing in these sections, we struggle to retain our grasp on the argument's intricacies. Our guide is (sometimes) a trickster, and he works hard to keep us on our toes. And he has big, scary surprises for us. Like the poem's denouement, for instance, where he suddenly hurls us smack into the middle of the Athenian plague, and leaves us there to find our own way out of it (using, theoretically, the survival skills our trickster has been teaching us). This cluster of subversive pedagogics disrupts the grand unity of the text, thus making the learning of its truths harder but sounder. We can repair that disorder spatially by making maps, in the manner suggested by Dalzell, of its 'architecture'. But the poet's thematic harmonics are, within the space of the text, as temporal as his dialogue with his reader. In his manipulation of his themes and their variations his mode is not so much philosophical as it is musical.

Several crucial themes inform the poem, and different readers emphasise different ones. The theme I find at the core of the poem is that of Destruction and Regeneration (Dalzell 1998, 69-70; Jenkyns 226-8). Atoms whirling endlessly in their Void: that is the essential truth of atomism. The End of This Planet – that, humanly speaking, is an essential corollary of the essential truth. Looked at from this perspective, the truth of atomism and all the truths one derives from it would seem to be bleak to the point of nihilism, and many readers of the poem, as we shall presently see, have tended to read the *DRN* in precisely this way. But Lucretius is, famously and infamously (depending on when and where you live), the poet, par excellence, of pleasure. If his worldview seems at first glance an odd alloy of futility and exuberant meliorism, we need to look more closely, and when we do what we find is something similar to Gramsci's precise moral formula: 'pessimism of the intellect, optimism of the will.' The poet is speaking here of our origin and our condition:

> We are all sprung from heavenly seed. All alike have the same father, from whom all-nourishing mother earth receives the showering drops of moisture. Thus fertilised, she gives birth to smiling crops and lusty trees, to mankind and all the breeds of beasts. She it is that yields the food on which they all feed their bodies, lead their joyous lives and renew their race. She has well earned the name of mother. (2.991-8)

The passage recalls the splendid opening of the poem in which the poet, disbeliever though he is in the gods of the poets and theologians and the state, nevertheless invokes Venus, as the inspiration, as the Muse, of his poem. Illusory though she may be, theologically speaking, she is, allegorically speaking, an exact *example* of how to shape one's habits of mind and heart, because (I sometimes think of her as a sort of music video featuring the shifting faces and smiles of Sophia Loren, *the* picture of Neapolitan fertility, wit, variety, vitality, awash in a rendition of Carl Orff's *Trionfo di Afrodite*) she incarnates (in myth, in artistic representations) the process of Nature, its unending espousal of 'desire and freedom' (Asmis 464: 'as an allegorical rival to the Stoic Zeus, she stands for pleasure and a world ordered by spontaneous impulses', 459).

But she also stands for Nature's dynamic of undoing and doing, of breaking and making. In this mode, she is more like the Great Mother, Cybele, whose worship the poet evokes in a dazzling passage (2.589-643) only to reject her, the Mother of Wild Beasts and the *genetrix* of humankind, when he reminds us that the earth is not, in fact, a female deity (644-54). Like us, the earth is made of atoms, it (not she) doesn't know or care about us. 'The reason why it sends up countless products in countless ways into the sunlight is simply that it contains atoms of countless substances' (653-4). When we think of the earth mother, it is

27

usually in her benign aspect. We want to forget that she takes away at least as much as she gives. The pictures of the Good Mother (Venus, Terra, Cybele, Ceres, Flora) are as useful as they are charming: provided they are not permitted to morph back from elegant allegory into corrupting superstition, they help us to remember that Nature creates no less than it destroys. At its simplest, the truth of the atoms is (or seems) too hard to bear if we focus entirely on the disintegrations. What we need to fix in our heads is the dialectic of creation/destruction, and this sometimes means holding fast to the images of fertility that the figure of Venus incarnates. Pondering Venus makes us look for the whole truth (Amory 157-9, 168).

Atomic truth may tell us that 'Everything is on the move. Everything is transformed by nature and forced into new paths. One thing, withered by time, decays and dwindles. Another grows strong and emerges from ignominy', (5.830-4); atomic truth may insist that things 'are generated from other things and retransformed into them, since it is an established fact that everything is in perpetual flux' (5.279-80). We may be – and we are – atoms cascading through the void, and we may be standing or walking on atoms cascading through the void, but we feel solid and we feel that we stand or walk on solid earth. We need be able to live our lives (joyfully) *as if* the solidities and permanences that our commonsense imagines and our instinct wants were realities (they are 'real', of course, and they are even, relatively speaking, durable ones; but we want them to be – imperishable). As the poet has told us, we don't really care about how many times the universes have been destroyed and created before this one that we live in; we inevitably care about this one, about the earth and the good (pleasant) necessities it provides us with. So we do feel like the children of the earth (and the starry sky). There is nothing wrong with that and with other similar feelings unless they become so powerful that we allow them to create new gods, both kindly and cruel, unless we permit politicians to find new ways of using our feelings about these gods to control what we think and what we do. But to be grateful to the earth, to rejoice in its variety and plenty, to love life and the good things life can give us – what's wrong with that? That's what the poem has come into existence to persuade us of:

After the natal season of the world, the birthday of sea and lands and uprisings of the sun, many atoms have been added from without, many seeds contributed on every side by bombardment from the universe at large. From these the sea and land could gather increase: the dome of heaven could gain more room and lift its rafters high above the earth, and the air could climb upwards. From every corner of the universe atoms are being chipped and circulated to each thing according to its own kind: water goes to water, earth swells with earthy matter; fire is forged by fires, ether by ether. At length everything is brought to its utmost limit of growth by nature, the creatress and perfectress. (2.1105-17).

After this moment, when nature has put her finishing touches on her earthly work, decline sets in. The logic of Empedocles is unpersuadable: Love and Strife, Strife and Love, their perpetual dynamic. We rejoice in the birth and growth, we dread the decadence, we fear the end (for we guess, as some wit once quipped, that there's night at the end of the tunnel). But, by constantly emphasising the dialectic of birth/death, by emphasising this theme so frequently in his opening books, particularly at the close of Book 2, Lucretius reminds us that the end of the story is not ours to know or to change. We are in the middle of the story, and, barring dreadful social inequities and other forms of bad luck (for instance, the plague), we do have some degree of say in whether that middle will be absolutely wretched or in some degree delightful, painful or pleasant, illusory or genuine. In the passage about the foul, leaky vessel in Book 6 the poet sings: 'No, the fault will be in you!' (73). That is: If you can't learn to see the gods as they are and imitate their equanimity and feel the joy they feel when they look at things as they are, if you can't accept your place in this brief eternity (in the middle of the story) and accept it joyfully, if you can't live in the light that Epicurus has discovered for us, then, blind to the dialectic of regeneration/destruction, ignorant of your life's real beginnings, oblivious to the wonderment of its middle, then, like Memmius when he understands the truth of atomism only at the apocalypse, you will finally seem to yourself to have gathered all your life up into a single moment, to have wound all your resentments, regrets and remorse into a tight spool – you will live your whole life only at its bitter end. But if you have perused the first two books of the

29

DRN and have pondered them carefully, if you have succeeded in making them your own, then that dialectic can indeed remake you. And you can learn to live, difficult thought it sounds, simultanously in the (unhuman) truth of the flux of the cascading world and in the substantial (human) middle of your story. The joyful wisdom of that pleasant paradox is what the poem is mostly 'about'.

Lust and love in the late Republic

What is that human middle of the story like? That is to say, once the mechanisms that distort our perceptions and our representations of them have been repaired, how do we live our human lives in the flux of atoms? The truth of atomism is, doubtless, important in and of itself, but this is a Roman asking the question, a person for whom the notions of 'pure knowledge' or 'truth for the sake of truth' sound slightly bogus. Humanly (or Romanly) speaking, it is what that truth produces, what it does to us and for us, that matters. What does it mean to be human in a godless world of godless atoms?

Lacking biographical data, lacking specific statements (like those of St Augustine, for example, or those of Rousseau or Malcolm X), we can only guess why the poet needed to pose that question so urgently, but in making those guesses we want to keep in mind the role that tensions in the poet's community and its collective (un)consciousness may have played in moving him to dissect human nature and reassemble it as he did.

In the decade Cicero read the *DRN* at his brother's urging, Julius Caesar was up in Gaul, dividing it, with the help of his increasingly unbeatable army, into three parts, and writing his elegant and chilling war memoirs, in which he perfects the theory and practice of genocide. The citizens of the Roman Republic were no longer able to ignore the widening fissures at its base. Their matchless armies, once composed of the citizen-farmer-soldiers who had won the empire and built the roads which traversed it, were becoming increasingly professional even as they became increasingly more loyal to the generals who led them than they were to the Roman people and the magistrates who (theoretically) represented them. The magistrates themselves, and the rich, venerable families they came from, had gradually forgotten how to share the profits of empire effectively with each other, with

30

their soldiers and the Roman people and their Italian allies. This military oligarchy, to call the system by its real name, had outgrown the institutions that had served it so well in its glory days; it could not, despite the efforts of progressives and conservatives alike (on the one hand, the brothers Gracchi, on the other, Cicero), accommodate itself to the reforms that might have saved it. Its favourite self-remedy, civil war, finally destroyed it.

No less subversive of the traditional sign system (the institutions and cultural repertoire that represented how the military oligarchy viewed itself and wanted itself viewed) was the growth in the political and cultural power of provincials. At the beginning of the last century of the Republic, Rome had almost been defeated by a coalition of its Italian allies (these 'Social Wars' are better called the Wars with the Allies); the aftermath of this near-defeat entailed in part an altered demography for the city of Rome, which became less Roman and more Italian just at the moment when it was also becoming, more and more, with each passing decade, a magnet for peoples from all over the Mediterranean world. The official language would remain Latin, but in the streets of Rome one heard a hundred other tongues. The city was getting ready to become the cosmopolis of the world empire that Julius Caesar had dreamed of and that his heir, Augustus, would realise (the city is also morphing into the spacetimes of Petronius' Trimalchio and of Juvenal's Malcontents). Meanwhile, the ideology of the military oligarchy (whose group portrait is the centre of Livy's vivid history) is getting ready to dwindle into myth and ritual, and the peculiar experiment in representative government, which had been based on a peculiar push-pull of winning and losing political and economic rights by the lower orders, of class struggle for social entitlement, of secession (general strike) by the have-nots, of defection by and co-option of Italian allies, all this based on a progressive awareness that 'where part of the real strength is, there also part of the real power' ought to be, *ubi pars virium, ibi et imperii pars esto*, Livy, 8.4 – all that, after four centuries of blood, sweat and tears, was closing down (Minyard 13-22, 70-9).

In Bakhtin's *The Dialogic Imagination* such periods of radical transition from one dominant ideology to another are held to be marked by huge linguistic and literary diversity. From a conservative perspective, these moments seem chaotic: the comforting voices that represent

31

'traditional values' and fading ideologies become shrill while the new voices, representing emerging or marginal or previously suppressed ideologies, sound crude, raucous, unintelligible. By the time a new dominant ideology is formed out of these competing voices and perspectives, the language of the vanished society has altered along with the political and cultural institutions that shaped that language and that in turn were shaped by it. The old 'monoglossia' of the old society has been replaced, after a period of 'heteroglossia' and its revolutions and carnivals, by a new 'monoglossia' for and of the new dominant ideology and its new regime and its new political (un)consciousness. This sketch of Bakhtin's model effaces its subtleties and ignores the fact (which the model does not) that societies and their languages are always in the process of being gradually transformed as well as being, on occasion, explosively transformed. For my immediate purposes, the crude sketch will do: when Lucretius was writing the *DRN* his society and his language were, for a variety of reasons, in the throes of a violent transformation that induced people to start asking themselves what it meant (*now*) to be (a) a Roman and (b) a human being. The history that Livy would be writing in the generation after Lucretius, a serious historical novel for grown-ups, tried to examine the question of whether the great men and the soldier-farmer-citizens they had led into battle against Hannibal and Rome's other enemies still mattered, were still valid models for the coming generations of Rome. He wanted to ask Romans if Rome was still Roman. (For Livy, now, see Zbigniew Herbert's brilliant poem, 'Transformations of Livy', in his *Elegy for the Departure*, trs. John and Bogdana Carpenter.)

In what does my humanity consist? And how does that humanity accord with what remains of my Roman self? While Lucretius worked on his poem, one of his contemporaries, the poet Catullus, was busy reframing these questions in the language that interested him most, the syntax and rhetoric of the erotic self. Another contemporary, the philosopher and statesman Cicero, also happens to have touched, reluctantly, on this topic. And it was one that Lucretius thought crucial to his entire project: a puritan hedonist can hardly avoid it since the links between self and desire reveal themselves in erotics vividly (if not clearly). The point where these three perspectives on Love's pains and pleasures collide offers an interesting vantage on the psychology of Lucretian man.

32

1. No Truth But in Atoms

Early in Act 1 of Tom Stoppard's *The Invention of Love*, a brilliant meditation on the scholar/poet A.E. Housman, Catullus is credited with having invented 'the love poem, ... the true-life confessions of the poet in love ... in Rome in the first century before Christ'. Contemporary students of Catullus doubt that he revealed his actual erotic raptures and mishaps in his poems, and they can point to various earlier literary representations of erotic obsession that he used as ingredients in his unique concoction. Even his most famous whine *de coeur*, poem 85, smells less of the boudoir than of the library:

> I hate, I love!
> You ask me maybe, How you manage that?
> Search me, pal,
> But I feel it coming on me,
> And it's wrenching me apart,
> Like a slave on a cross.

Yet for all its genuinely literary provenance and its manifest textuality, the Catullan book achieves 'an illusion of reality' that easily seduces its common readers into believing that they have encountered the real thing: a man in love who happens to be a poet. Partly it does this because Catullus insists on naming himself and his friends in the poems, on putting himself and them in moments and places that smack of 'real life'. His deft repetitions of and variations on this sense of 'daily life' and social exchange induce us to fashion a linear story for these scattered instances of an imaginary life that art renders 'real'. But there is something else. Though only Catullus' poems have survived for us intact (poems by his contemporaries, some of them his friends, have vanished almost without trace), it's pretty clear that the decades that comprised Catullus' life saw a remarkable ferment in the production of romantic-and-erotic verse (and there were inklings of this ferment in the generation just before his). Hence, it's possible that some of the power and clarity of this erotic presence, this testament to erotic truth and erotic value, derives from something like a collective (un)consciousness in these poets and their readers, one which centres itself on an awakening erotic novelty, on new and different erotic roles. I'm not talking here of 'sexual revolution', but of a Bakhtinian tremor that becomes a small earthquake.

In the glory days of the Republic, at the centre of erotic ideology was, naturally, the phallos, whose message was, Fathers Know Best and Fathers Fuck Whom They Please. By and large, however, they saved their precious fluids for the family gene-pool, they were mostly monogamous, and their sexual appetites were held firmly in check (at least in theory) and were essentially governed by the idea of procreation. But in Catullus' day, the figure of Father, which is closely intertwined with political and economic ideologies, is wearing thin. The biggest, ugliest icon of Roman Fatherhood is perhaps the consul Manlius (Livy 8.7) who subordinates paternal feeling to patriotic duy and orders the execution of his own son who had, in a burst of heroism or vanity or both, against orders, prematurely engaged the enemy. That was then (the fourth century BCE), but now, when Catullus and his friends are in their heyday, their motto is: Fathers Knew Best. Plentifully mixed with his erotic verses are Catullus' funny, dirty musings on contemporary politics. In this part of his factual-fictional self-portrait-in-cityscape, he resembles the dour young men in nineteenth-century Russian novels who are cynics getting ready to become anarchists. The role models for political careers have crumbled, the patterns for erotic behavior are vanishing. If the poetry of Catullus is any index, his generation especially, along with some of his older and younger contemporaries, represent a once taciturn, invisible minority who are in the process of becoming a vocal, conspicuous minority.

Much of the symbolic (and even some of the material) paraphernalia of the Roman *paterfamilias* will persist as long as Rome is ruled by Romans (and some of it persists in Western tradition still, not least in the Vatican), but in the late Republic various people who wanted new erotic patterns, and came upon them while other social patterns were breaking up, needed and found poets who would tell them that it's a very good thing to go crazy for a love that may destroy you but that will, in the process, transform your humdrum, vapid existence into a Life, into something so delicious and so profound and so expansive that any and every pain and humiliation it costs will seem a bargain once the fatal transaction is completed.

This style of paradisiacal love is an addiction. In a particularly well-wrought poem (72), as intense as any passive-aggressive lament in the Country & Western repertoire, we find the lover no longer asking his girlfriend to love him back or to abandon her promiscuity;

instead he begs the gods to release him from his disgusting sickness. He wants to be healthy. We know they won't do that, because we know (as does he) that he's not sincere in his supplication. He wants to die as he has loved (lived), a prisoner of erotic illusion and a prince of pleasure, including the refined pleasure of self-abasement. When the lover snatches (in poem 99) 'a kisslet sweeter than sweet ambrosia' from his boyfriend, Juventius, he doesn't get off scot-free. The young man washes his lips and rubs them dry 'as if they had been smeared with the spittle of a sick whore', he refuses forgiveness to his lover, who is 'nailed high on the cross', until he promises that he will kiss no more (unless permission is granted). The thief of kisses, the master of erotic aggression, slinks off with his tail between his legs, thwarted, humiliated, nullified – and in seventh heaven!

He hates and he loves, he is wasting his life, he needs to shake the habit, he needs to learn just to say no (to himself and to his girl- and boyfriends). But he also needs to snatch more of those kisses, to climb higher (and more spectacular) crosses (and to write more poems). He needs – it is a vicious circle, devoutly to be wished. Becoming the slave of one's desire is fascinating and it gives one something exciting and readily available to do. It also distracts one's attention from the ruin of the city and the dwindling opportunies for achieving traditional (and obsolete) manhood. If it is perilous and futile, it is also very beautiful and lots of fun.

Cicero thought otherwise. The new fashion (he didn't guess – or did he? – that this style of erotic self-fashioning would have a long history, one that does not culminate in Madame Bovary, one that can be exported from the West) struck him as a mere variation on an old theme, the madness of love, which his favorite Greeks (Athenian, Plato's version of the fifth century, in short, Classical) had understood so well (as they understood everything: except how to rule the world). For those wisest of men, Eros (Amor) was a sort of demon who inflicted temporary, if sometimes fatal, madness, especially on those who were poorly educated or had some marked character flaw. (Even the wisest could succumb, of course, but generally these people came to their senses in time, before something dreadful happened to them and their community.) Cicero claimed that if he should be given another lifetime he would still not have time enough to read lyric love poetry.

There is little or no evidence that he read Catullus, but he was aware of him and his friends and voiced his dislike for their stylistic experiments. But he was doubtless no less repelled by their content and their contempt for 'old values'. Certainly, the emphasis put by these poets on love in general and neurotic lovers in particular could not expect to earn them his approbation (many of these poets are listed by Ovid in his *Tristia* 2, including a certain Memmius, a writer of erotic verse, who might be our Memmius). Pliny the Younger, it's true (*Epistles* 7.4.4-6), tells of reading some light verse of Cicero addressed to his private secretary, Tiro, in which kisses not so dissimilar from the Catullan variety would seem to have cut some figure. But light verse and lover's kisses are not prominent in Cicero's extant writings, nor are they compatible with the stern judgment he passes on Love and Sex.

Catullus knows about 'rationality' and 'free will', and when his foot is on the edge of the abyss, he seems ready to invoke them, to want to recoup them and find shelter in them from his madness. But we never quite believe him when he toys with the possibility of being restored to rationality and sound volition: he is the hero (our hero) of transcendental eroticisim, and we know he won't fail us (though we may intone pious regrets for his predicament, under our breath we are muttering, Jump, baby, jump). Cicero has no time for the erotomaniac's nostalgia for mental health or for the myth of moderate sensuality that may be thought to fuel it (as if Catullus and company were saying, If only I could learn to be half-horny):

> Anyone that talks of finding a 'limit' to vice might as well suppose that the scapegoat criminal flung annually from the promontory on the island of Leucas could decide to suspend his fall in mid-air. He can't do it, and neither can a distempered psyche, one in the grip of its vice, get hold of itself and halt its plummet. (*Tusculan Disputations* 4.41)

All disruptions of the natural functions of the psyche have their origins in voluntary decisions based on misinterpretations of what should be really feared and what should be really desired (4.82). But there are degrees of disruption, and finally there is even a change from the quantitative to the qualitative when the creature in question passes from peccadillos to sinful madness. Some people are disoriented by their misreadings of what they should fear or desire and lose their ability to keep their thoughts and emotions in some sort of balance, but some people utterly surrender themselves (like cowardly soldiers) to what began as a minor ailment and ends as a fatal, disgusting sickness: these are the leprous damned (and Catullus, along with people who style themselves Epicureans, is doubtless among them). This yielding to the sickness is unspeakable; it is the source of all wretchedness. Yet even this sickness can be healed by what alleviates the minor, preliminary illnesses that can lead to it. The single, sure cure is effected when the sufferer is forced to admit that all his troubles have come to him because he willingly consented to act according to his own misconceptions of what most pained and what most pleasured him (4.83).

All this sounds not a little like Lucretius' leaky bucket, and it is certainly true that Cicero and Lucretius (like most post-Platonic philosophers) are deeply concerned with the problem of pain and pleasure in its links with the problem of doing the right thing and living a (or *the*) good life. But this is a deceptive unanimity. If their cures for the root causes of human discontent sound similar (truth will make you sane), the answers they give to the problems they share are different (Cicero's pragmatic idealism vs. Lucretius' ethical hedonism), and they also differ widely in how they view erotic excess and in how they go about defining its place in human nature.

Cicero begins his account by trying to distinguish between lust as ailment and lust as fatal disease. 'Those who feel blissful when they are having sex we call "immoral", but those who crave their fornications with every fibre of their being we call "profligate" (4.68). Having made this distinction, he doubts the need for it. 'This thing commonly called "love" – is there, God help us, a synonym for it that might serve us as a euphemism? Any and every variety of it is so trivial that I'm hard pressed to think of any thing that rivals it in worthlessness.' Poets make much of it. Tragedians and comedians both, as well as lyricists, find it attractive material (naturally, it deals with emotions that are huge and violent), and they even show the gods, even Jupiter himself, as engaged in this dirty game (70). If that were not enough, even philosophers have endorsed L-O-V-E. At this point, things gets so crazy that the only philosopher we find who is speaking the truth is Epicurus (he describes 'love' as a hankering for genital activities). The

37

others find good things to say about it. It is, for instance, the beginning of friendship. You bet! If that's the case, how come no one ever falls in love with a really ugly adolescent or with a cute old fart? The Greek philosophers seem to have derived their notion of loving friendship from their experiences in the gymnasia where 'that sort of love was free and legal'. The Roman poet Ennius gives the lie to that myth when he reminds us that when men start stripping in front of each other for exercise strange thoughts begin popping into their heads. Cicero supposes that such loves could be put on a leash, but by and large they seem to cause more trouble than they're worth.

This train of thought troubles him. He tries to break it off, but: 'Furthermore, not to mention love affairs with women, to which Nature is more lenient', (he really says this) 'is anyone uncertain of what is going on when Ganymede is whisked into the skies or when the father of Oedipus, in the play, explains his particular preferences?' (71) Other pederasts flash onto his memory screen: Alcaeus, Anacreon, and (worst of them all) Ibycus. All of these examples show that when people say Love they mean Lust. Even his beloved Plato has accorded Love a special place in the moral realm, and so have the usually dependable Stoics who confer on Lust a crucial role in the making of the wise man. This bothers him, he falters. 'If,' he cries, 'if in the nature of things there is such a pure love, a love that is the foundation of friendship and of wisdom, a pattern of goodness, a love that is without anxiety and raw yearning and fretting and heavy breathing – if there is, well and good!' Cicero is not talking about that ideal entity, he's talking about the psyche's erotic gyrations and disequilibriums. So he wants us to use some other word when we're trying to talk about the good kind of love. (We won't do that if we keep on reading those Platonic dialogues where the wisest of the wise are ogling their apprentices.)

What is the cure for lechery, for what the world calls love (that's his formal question, but he is specially concerned with same-sexual obsessions)? You have to reveal to the patient how worthless what he craves really is. You have to explain to him that what he's after can be got elsewhere or in a different way (screwing slaves, masturbation?), or that the desire for it can be utterly shut out from the brain. Then there are other interests, hobbies, obligations, various diversions. He can also travel. He must especially be reminded that love is a madness, is in fact the worst madness because the mad lover uses reason to destroy reason. Finally, you have to convince the lunatic that every instant of the amatory life he has misled has been shaped by powerful misconceptions which his corrupt volition has ratified. What this means is that Love (as the poets and philosophers join with the great unwashed in calling it) is not 'natural' at all. 'If love were "natural", everyone would be a lover and they would always be in love and the objects of their affection would be the same, and you wouldn't find one lover ashamed of his love, another inclined to mull it over, another gorged on it' (76). (Maybe he *has* been reading Catullus, after all.) True philosophers have thought love over and become ashamed of it. They have seen that it is not natural, at least not as practised by most people, that vocal majority who insist on its naturalness. It is a rather filthy instinct for propagation that we share with other animals; unlike those animals, however, we can learn to transcend it by suppressing it. Whatever exists in nature that culture and reason cannot remake or tame must be extinguished. Lust, what various people, whether ignorantly deluded or cynically deluding, call love, is one of these expendables. Not necessary except for breeders, not natural except for beasts and madmen and criminals.

This is a perdurable, always recurrent human perspective, and Cicero's spin on it has, in the tradition of Western erotics, not lacked influence. It makes the perspective of Catullus (which in Cuba they sometimes name *el amor de loca juventud*) look pretty good.

Lucretius distils desire

At first blush, Lucretius seems to be in Cicero's corner. A reading of the end of Book 4, however, shows that his verdict, as one might expect, is closer to 'A plague on both your houses.' The disquisition on sex (which does indeed contain a tirade against erotic obsession) concludes Book 4's discussion of questions of perception and sensation. In describing the mechanism of images in dreams, the poet remarks that little boys often wet their beds as they dream themselves standing over a chamberpot. As teenagers they encounter another problem:

> Those boys in whom the seed is for the first time working its way into the choppy waters of their youth are invaded from without by images emanating from some body or other with tidings of an

alluring face and a delightful complexion. This stimulates the organs swollen with an accumulation of seed. Often, as though their function were actually fulfilled, they discharge a flood of fluid and stain their clothes. (4.1030-6)

Poor kids, if they but knew what deeper humiliations lay in store for them later when fiercer images come steadily to assault them, transforming them into a kind of perpetual love engine. 'When a man is pierced by the shafts of Venus, whether they are launched by a lad with womanish limbs or a woman radiating love from her whole body, he strives towards the source of the wound and craves to be united with it and to ejaculate the fluid drawn from out of his body into that body' (1054-6). When he is in this condition (as he usually is) – all those images bombarding his eyeballs, all that sperm pulsating in his groin, all those memories of past pleasures churning in his head – he becomes a brute beast, he loses his capacity for reasoned speech (1057), and the only voice he hears in his brain is the voice of his penis, promising bliss. He is heading for the Epicurean goal, pleasure, and (Cicero be damned!) his movement towards pleasure in general and *this* pleasure in particular is eminently natural. But this version of this pleasure is the wrong version.

It is at this point in his discussion that the poet turns his attention to Catullus & Company: 'This, then, is what we term Venus. This is the origin of the thing called love – that drop of Venus' honey that first drips into our heart to be followed by an icy heartache' (1058-60). To paraphrase: 'We, today, call it love, or rather, various people, poets leading the pack, have begun to give the word Love a new meaning. They have begun saying love when they mean lust, as if love and lust were identical, as if lust were love's best synonym.' The next hundred and thirty lines or so will be devoted to showing how this piece of sophistry works and to indicating how it deconstructs itself.

In Catullan love, the lover is bewitched by a phantom, an incarnation of his own desire. You can fight against this huge error by fleeing images that set it in motion. You can also help matters by using the technique recommended by Diogenes (jerking off) or by Horace (grabbing the first slave you can lay your hands on). If you keep your sperm inside you as long as you are possessed by the image of your desire (you call her or him, my beloved), your desire will fester as it grows, and your madness will keep pace with that growth. Your only hope, then, is a series of one night stands (*volgivagaque vagus Venere*, 1071). This is obviously the kind of advice that neither Catullus nor Cicero cares to hear. For Catullus, it cheapens the meaning of romantic love; for Cicero it destroys the purity of body and of mind. But for Lucretius (who here stands firmly in the Cynic tradition) it is pure common-sense. Cicero had said, Think of other things, just say no. Catullus had said, Think of none but the beloved, say yes only to her or him. Lucretius says:

> Do not think that by avoiding romantic love you are missing the delights of sex. Rather, you are reaping the sort of profits that carry with them no penalty. Rest assured that this pleasure is enjoyed *in a purer form by the sane than by the lovesick* [the italics are mine]. They cannot make up their mind what to enjoy first with eye or hand. They clasp the objects of their longing so tightly that the embrace is painful. They kiss so fiercely that teeth are drawn into lips. All this because their pleasure is not pure, but they are goaded by an underlying impulse to hurt the thing, whatever it may be, that gives rise to those budding shoots of madness. (1078-83)

I doubt that Lucretius is really insisting that sex be demure (that it won't get a little vigorous when the spirit moves us); rather, he is equating obsessive romantic love with an aggressive frenzy whose object is not sexual satisfaction but the blind need for something that is part cruel domination, part revenge for earlier dissatisfactions. The mad lover expects that his passion will be extinguished by what called it into being, but 'this runs clean counter to the course of nature. This is the one thing of which the more we have, the more our breast burns with the evil lust (*dira cupido*) of having' (1088-90). Our desire for food and drink can be easily satisfied; in the right way, so can our sexual needs, but they are more mysterious than hunger and thirst, and, because they are as much or more mental than they are physical (a point for Cicero), because they gravitate toward a sort of superstitious obsession with *the one sure, best source of getting this pleasure again*, they are more difficult to understand and to master: 'A pretty face or a pleasing complexion gives the body nothing to enjoy but insubstan-

41

tial images which all too often pathetic hope scatters to the wind'
(1094-6).

It is this erotic lightshow of prospective partners, a sort of constant
porn show in the mind, that accounts for the mad lover's delusions and
for the futility and frenzy that they engender. Just at the moment of
orgasm:

> body clings greedily to body; they mingle the saliva of their
> mouths and breathe hard down each other's mouths pressing
> them with their teeth. But all to no purpose. One can remove
> nothing from the other by rubbing, nor enter right in and be
> wholly absorbed, body in body; for sometimes it seems that that
> is what they are craving to do, so hungrily do they cling together
> in Venus' fetters, while their limbs are unnerved and liquefied by
> the intensity of pleasure. (1108-16)

As we will presently see, Lucretius has as little against orgasm as he
has against French kisses. The problem is not that these lovers
experience carnal raptures. The problem is that these mad lovers (or
one variety of them, the Catullan adepts) are trying to satisfy a purely
mental obsession by a physical act which is natural and, if not necessary, all but inevitable. But what bothers Lucretius most here is that
a perfectly good pleasure is being spoiled by neurotic cravings for
illusory pleasures that bring trouble and ruin along with them. Good
sex may not be, for Lucretius, the best pleasure, but he knows that it
is one of the easiest available and, properly satisfied, also one of the
most reliable (as well as being, for many, the most delightful: Lucretius
would not mind hearing it called 'the poor man's opera'). It is because
he knows the value of good sex that he can say, without prudery, in a
way that Cicero could not: 'In starved and unrequited love the evils
you can plainly see without opening your eyes are past all counting.
How much better to be on your guard beforehand, as I have advised,
and take care that you are not enmeshed' (1142-5). Take care, that is,
not to be enmeshed in romantic lust. Plain lust (or, as we'll soon see,
married lust) is another matter. But before he turns to the nature of
fulfilled and requited love, he offers Catullan lovers one last piece of
free advice and launches into his rendition of the catalogue of the
euphemisms that crazy Don Juans bestow on their beloveds, a page

from the rhetoric of erotics in which the loved one's defects, physical and psychological, become virtues (if she is coughing her lungs up, she is 'delicate'). In revealing how this rhetoric self-implodes (to expose its folly all he has to do is provide a few examples of it), he both knots up his central condemnation of bad love and repeats, with new emphasis, his recipe for escape from bad love. Since it is images of desire we use to create phantasms of our beloveds, in order to free ourselves from our obsessions we must defabricate those images, we must learn to see how and why they are produced (with our help).

The catalogue is not misogynistic, the poet is not making fun of women. He is making fun of the myth and cult of perfect beauty, and he is especially ridiculing men who promote that illusion in order to sentimentalise their lusts while forcing women to be complicit with them in that masculine erotic project: no compliance from them, no material rewards for them. The human body (male, he knows, as well as female) is not usually very enticing without help of baths (at the least). Part of the process of sustaining the cult and myth involves the use of cosmetics to hide what is unpleasant (another part: to create the illusion that spectacular beauty does not come out of a bottle). Women make sure we don't know much about their beauty secrets. If we take the trouble to investigate those secrets we will not come to feel disgust at women, but we will learn something more about how to defabricate romantic images and so lessen their hold on us. He concludes this section on the power of the beauty industry and its devotees with a dry, wry remark. All the pains bestowed on cosmetics are wasted 'since your mind has power to drag all these mysteries into the daylight and get at the truth behind all the giggling. Then, if the woman is good-hearted and void of malice it is up to you to turn to accept unpleasant facts and make allowance for human imperfection' (4.1188-91). That may sound sexist, but the poet knows that a good way of beginning to accept unpleasant facts and make allowances for human imperfections is to first look in the mirror. If love is what you're after, you will want realities. What matters is what kind of woman she is: *si bello animost et non odiosa*. 'Of good disposition,' says one commentator for *bellus animus*, but let's give Lucretius the benefit of the doubt. Maybe he means a beautiful spirit, one that it is not tainted by ugly feelings. Maybe he means very congenial, *simpatica*; maybe he even means a woman with equanimity to match (one hopes) one's own (Godwin Book IV, 8, 165, 169-70).

And if you find this unmythical and everyday paragon, if you are able to get her to bed or even to the altar, then what happens? Don't pay any attention to what your male relatives or your army buddies may have told you. Women can come, they do come, and they even like to come.

> Do not imagine that a woman is always sighing with feigned love when she clings to a man in close embrace, body to body, and prolongs his kisses by the tension of moist lips. Often she is acting from the heart and is longing for a shared delight when she stimulates him to run love's race to the end. (1192-6)

In other words, don't be selfish, pal. The student may find this difficult to believe, so the poet backs it up with some examples from the farmyard. And in case the reader still refuses to entertain the notion that pure, good lust is available in and compatible with monogamy or the marriage bed, in case he thinks that real sex is to be had only with one's fantasy beloved or with skilled professionals in back alleys, not with one's ordinary helpmeet, the satirist caps this section of his argument with a neat cartoon:

> How often dogs at a street corner, wishing to separate, tug lustily with all their might in opposite directions, and yet remain united by the constraining fetters of Venus? This they would never do unless they knew the mutual joys which could entice them into the trap and hold them enchained. Here there is proof on proof for my contention that the pleasure of sex is shared. (1201-8)

Birds and cattle and dogs all do it, lust is lust the world round. I believe he knows his final proof is surreal. It's a good way to end the section that deals with sex as sex. Married sex, like animal sex, is natural and (essentially) necessary. It does not need poetry to glamorise it (or degrade it). Ciceronian sex, of course, is never funny. And Catullan sex, though it may stumble from camp tragedy into farcical melodrama, is never funny either. At the streetcorner, in the barnyard, in the marriage bed, that's where you find the giggles.

The poet has imagined us getting our ideal (that is to say, our compatible) mate. He has tucked us into bed, he has reminded us about the importance of mutual orgasm to a pleasant union. He then shifts to other matters. There are questions of genetic compatibility to think of (atoms have something to do with this, he's not sure what). Don't bother praying to the gods if you're having trouble with pregnancy. They don't concern themselves with these (or any) human matters. There are various difficulties in conception and various remedies for them. He offers some advice. Important is the position of intercourse. He recommends the position used by quadrupeds. The sexy contortions that hookers employ are useless, they're just trying not to get pregnant. 'Obviously our wives do not need any of them.' Because for them (and us) sex is for making children as well as having fun.

He likes children (they provide the poem with some of its loveliest imagery), and we get the sense that he likes the idea of fatherhood (Jenkyns 276). But it's not with the blessings of procreation that the poet ends his disquisition on the Joys of Sex:

> Lastly it is by no divine intervention, no prick of Cupid's darts that a woman deficient in beauty sometimes becomes the object of love. Often the woman herself, by her actions, by humouring a man's fancies and keeping herself fresh and smart, makes it easy for him to share his life with her. Over and above this, love is built up bit by bit by mere usage. Nothing can resist the continually repeated impact of a blow, however light, as you see drops of water falling on one spot at long last drill through a stone. (1278-87)

More about the woman's unspectacular looks, more about humouring your guy and keeping up your appearance (such as it is) for him. And then, there's the boredom of marriage, and there's something that sounds a bit like needing to be brainwashed to get through it. But I don't think that's the tone here. The crucial utterance is: *ut facile insuescat te secum degere vitam*. A shared life: sharing your life with her (as she shares hers with you). Lucretius has little to say about one of Epicurus' favourite themes, that of friendship. This marriage (or relationship) seems to qualify as a Lucretian version of what friendship might be and mean. As we shall see in the next chapter, Lucretius

45

makes sex and being married with children the catalyst of the start of civilisation (5.1011-18). Good sex, along with the realities and respon-sibilities that it entails, turns out to be one of the ways of fixing the leaky bucket. For that to happen, the phantasms and the images that foster them must be exorcised. It is a slow process, like water dripping on a stone, eroding the bad pictures and the bad passions they nourish. The human being who helps us do this (in bed and out of bed) is a friend indeed. And it is even possible that she may learn to look at us without wishing we were a bit more handsome, a little less dull, a little neater in our dress, had better table manners, paid her a bit more attention, liked foreplay a little more: trading patience. Neither Cicero nor Catullus (for different reasons) finds this woman in any way attractive. Lucretius does.

He likes it that by sharing his bed with her he is learning to share his life with her as well (whose bed is it, anyway? the question no longer matters). That means that he (an existing individual, a skinful of atoms in a world of zillions of atoms in their godless collisions) is not alone after all. He is really part of the wild and endless swarming of the atoms, but he is also, now, really rooted in his world and in his life. In the grand finale of Book 2 he had been made to confront the fact of Empedoclean (dis)harmony, the dialectic of creation and destruction, the sour truth of his and the world's decline and fall. So, in the majestic finale of Book 3, he was forced to face up to the 'bitter hug of mortality'. In this section of his poem, the poet ferociously rebukes the fake hedonism of Cecil B. DeMille movies and tombstone Paganism (Eat, drink and be merry, for tomorrow you must die) and replaces it with another style of wisdom: Unlearn extravagant fears of death, free yourself from them so you can learn to enjoy your life: that is, to greet gratefully the small (and carefully selected) pleasures of the senses and the big pleasures of truth. Finally, in Book 4's finale, Lucretian man has been exposed to the truth about his senses (their powers and their limitations), and he has been shown methods of distinguishing illusory desires from real ones. Now, his appetites chastened and sharpened and purified (and remember, he is, essentially, nothing but his appetites, a clustering of selfish atoms that want and need food, sleep, diversions, truth), he is ready to move on to other and in some ways even harder lessons.

2

The Gospel of Pleasure

As for Metropolis, that too great city; her illusions are not mine.

W.H. Auden

From beast to man

Lucretian man has just found a friendly wife to help him re-educate the erotic desires that, left to the mercy of erotic fashion (Cicero's or Catullus'), could ruin his pleasure in good sex, or waste his energies, or destroy his life. As a private person (one made of atoms and the void, one living in a godless world) he has found his footing. He knows the atomic truth: that he lives, briefly and insecurely, in a world which, though without a plan or a purpose, richly supplies his needs; he knows the vanity of his death-fears, the meaning of his mortality; he knows, too, the meaning of his carnality, the shape and limits of his desires; above all, he knows the spine-tingling pleasure of coming to understand the countless universes and how they work. What he doesn't know yet is how things became so muddled when humans began, out of necessity, to live together. He needs to find some way of becoming a public person without losing what he knows and is as a private person. What is the civilised world? And how can a Roman Epicurean live in it?

Those questions were urgent (in the poem and outside it) because the civilised world (Rome's) showed signs of buckling under the stresses it had created for itself. A perfected Epicurean might be able to face those stresses with the requisite fabled serenity. But an ordinary (commonsensical) Roman Epicurean would still want to ask himself, how do I live my life in such a world? What connection do I have with, what share do I have in, the (vanishing, changing) metropolis? The old answers to these old questions relied on outworn metaphysical underpinnings (as they mostly do still). Lucretius could

47

find no comfort in them, though others could or tried to. Even as Lucretius was rejecting those answers in his poem, Cicero was burnishing the old answers to a new brilliance that would shine, one of humanism's glories, for two millennia:

> That animal which we can call man, endowed with foresight and quick intelligence, complex, keen, possessing memory, full of reason and prudence, has been given a certain distinguished status by the supreme God who created him; for he is the only one among so many different kinds and varieties of living beings who has a share in reason and thought while all the rest are deprived of it. (tr. Clinton Walker Keyes, The Loeb Edition)

This is Cicero talking (*Laws* 1.22). He is getting ready to sketch his idea of natural law, an exquisite contraption in whose complexities the Deity, Mankind, Reason, Nature, Language, Truth and Justice, elegantly fuse. It is because man and gods (all of them obedient to 'the divine mind and the God of transcendent power') belong to the same commonwealth that Nature, the instrument of God,

> has lavishly yielded such a wealth of things adapted to man's convenience and use that what she produces seems intended as a gift to us, and not brought forth by chance; and this is true, not only of what the fertile earth bountifully bestows in the form of grain and fruit, but also of the animals; for it is clear that some of them have been created to be man's slaves, some to supply him with their products and others to serve as his food. Moreover, innumerable arts have been discovered through the teachings of nature; for it is by skilful imitation of her that reason has acquired the necessities of life. (25-6)

Nature has also given Man a body to match his mind: 'while she has bent the other creatures down toward their food, she has made man alone erect, and has challenged him to look up toward heaven, as being, so to speak, akin to him, and his first home' (26). Thus divinely fortified, Man is ready to go forth into the world (his oyster) divinely prepared for him. Cicero forgets to mention that large numbers of human beings share the fate of slavery with some animals, but other-

48

wise his description of this pristine Arcadia in which civilisation develops 'naturally' according to a godly design is as comprehensive as it is seductive. Human beings who are bad or stupid or both can and do disrupt this Panglossian perfection temporarily, but essentially our world is the best of all possible worlds because (unless we are slaves, or otherwise expendable and irrelevant) divine reason shaped us in his (not 'its') image for a spacetime that was precisely crafted for us.

Lucretius, as we've seen, yields to no one in his admiration of Nature's variety, vitality and beauty, but he has few illusions about its benevolence towards its creatures, let alone its partiality for humans. The first human beings, he says, 'were far tougher than the men of today, as became the offspring of tough earth' (5.925-6). For a long time 'they lived out their lives in the fashion of wild beasts roaming at large', they were 'content to accept as a free gift what the sun and showers had given and the earth had produced unsolicited', 'they did not know as yet how to enlist the aid of fire or to make use of skins'. 'They could have no thought of the common good, no notion of the mutual restraint of morals or laws', and it was 'mutual desire or the male's mastering might and profligate lust, or a bribe of acorns or arbutus berries or choice pears' that brought the sexes together (932, 937-8, 953-4, 957-8, 962-5). 'Thanks to their surpassing strength of hand and foot, they hunted the woodland beasts by hurling stones and wielding ponderous clubs. They were more than a match for many of them: from a few they took refuge in hiding-places' (966-9). They hunted by day, by night they hid from predators and slept. Surprisingly, not many more died then, devoured by wild beasts, seeing their own 'living flesh entombed in a living sepulchre', than die today (993). They didn't get medical aid if they needed it, but they also didn't march off in military formation to be slaughtered, they weren't drowned at sea while pursuing wealth. Sometimes they starved to death, to be sure, but they didn't perish from a surfeit of nourishment (as happens today), and though they sometimes accidentally poisoned themselves by eating the wrong plant, they didn't poison one another (as happens today).

This ironic constrast between that bestial *then* and our civilised *now* marks (and hides) a curious gap in what is about to become the poet's narrative of human progress. Those savages were not noble. They were wretched, they lived like beasts, in fact, they *were* beasts, but, at the same time, in some important ways, they were better off than we are (this antinomy, lucky/unlucky savages//lucky/unlucky us, haunts this narrative throughout and ties its final knot). What was it that made possible the transition from bestiality to humanity, from raw nature to refined culture, from wretchedness to the blessings of society? The poet doesn't tell us. 'As time went by, men began to build huts and to use skins and fire' (1011). 'As time went by' is a perfectly reasonable translation for *inde*, but it disguises the poet's careful indeterminacy, it fills in the blank that he leaves. What he says is: 'then' (what happened) or 'next'. Cicero would fill this blank with 'through the teachings of nature', and Lucretius will, in his next section, when he discusses the origins of language, have recourse to this metaphor ('As for the various sounds of spoken language, it was nature that drove men to utter these', 1028-9). But Lucretian nature is less a kind teacher than a brutal taskmaster. It is ferocious necessity that compels these humans to teach themselves, through desperate trial and error, how to find ways of not being destroyed by other beasts and by nature in its more threatening incarnations. How long did it take for these human beasts to learn how not to perish, to become technological beasts? How many had to die before the right lessons could be mastered? Lucretius doesn't say. He doesn't pretend to know the intricate history of mistakes and suffering that led finally to the discoveries that would make continued survival (of the fit and the fortunate) possible. That ignorance of the unknowable is properly acknowledged and dismissed with this 'next', 'then'. What Lucretius does know is that gods did not teach men to build huts or cure skins or make fires. Nor did an angelic Nature, messenger of the Divine Mind, bring down from heaven these miracles. Frightened beasts, suffering century after century, using their expanding brains, using their ever more agile thumbs, experimenting, failing, never quitting, finally stumbled upon what saved them. That's miracle enough for Lucretius (Dodds 20).

Married with children

But immediately after the miracle of huts, skins and fire, there comes another event, one hardly less miraculous. 'Woman mated with man, moved into a single home, and the laws of marriage were learnt as they

50

watched over their joint progeny' (1012). Driven by the threat of oblivion, man invents home and hearth, then has the idea of monogamy thrust upon him. From being a lonely brute (whether truly alone or in packs) he, our Adam, becomes married with children. These new arrangements produce new needs and values: 'Then it was that humanity first began to mellow. Thanks to fire, their chilly bodies could not longer so easily endure the cold under the canopy of heaven. Venus subdued brute strength' (1015-17). Began to mellow: cultural selection induces physical and psychological changes. There had been plenty of copulation out in the open in broad daylight, but now, as these men and women huddle together in their new huts, they learn to cuddle, to be affectionate with one another. This is a new Venus, a marriage goddess who diminishes the men's brutality (and maybe the women's, too?). They have learned to escape some of the pain that cold and inclement weather brings, they have discovered the pleasure of warm fires and warm beds and unhurried, playful sex. These people have the makings of Epicureans. They flee pain, they search for pleasure. Good technology and the ethical values that good technology can bring with it have begun to transform them from brutes to rational human beings.

But there is a further step in this initial transformation. We saw in the previous chapter how important procreation was in Lucretius' representation of the joys of good sex. Note here, too, that children have a crucial role in the new configuration of material practices and the emotional-intellectual habits they give rise to. The hut unites these men and women, their new style of lust-love also unites them, but what clinches their union is their joint responsibility for their offspring.

> Children by their wheedling easily broke down their parents' stubborn temper. The neighbours began to form mutual alliances, wishing neither to do nor to suffer violence among themselves. They appealed on behalf of their children and womenfolk, pointing out with gestures and inarticulate cries that it is right for everyone to pity the weak. (1018-23)

Coming in from the cold has tamed them, conjugal sex has tamed them more, and their children's charming pestering does the rest. They

51

want to protect their children. It is this powerful desire that forces them to make common cause with their neighbours. *This* social contract is forged from comfort and lust and ratified by the pleasures of parenthood.

Epicurus had suggested that people began to live in civilised groups when they agreed with one another neither to inflict nor to suffer harm. Lucretius puts a special (Italian?) spin on the master's insight by insisting that it is the values (and pleasures) of a husband and a father that are responsible for the ideas of *civitas* and *res publica*. 'Don't hurt my wife, don't hurt my kids (and I won't hurt yours). They are weak, we are strong. It is right (*aequum*, it is equal, fair, just) for everyone (who is strong) to feel compassion for those who are weak (*imbecillorum esse aequum misererier omnis*). I would feel pain if my wife and children were harmed by you; you would feel pain if I harmed your wife and children. In this matter, we can appreciate each other's pain and each other's pleasure.' Justice is here linked with compassion, both of which become intelligible from the perspective offered by the dialectic of pain and pleasure. I'm not suggesting that this is the best version of ethics (though I happen to feel that it may be), I'm merely sketching what seems to me to be the meaning of Lucretius' idea of how cities and justice and compassion come into being. Pleasure here is certainly the absence of pain ('I experience pleasure when my loved ones are not harmed by you'); but this negative form of pleasure is better understood as the condition of a larger economy of pleasure: 'I want to be able to enjoy my hearth and home, I want to enjoy being with my wife and kids.'

Pure necessity (escape from the perils of the cold, dark world) has joined with lust to produce a powerful configuration of desires and values and moral institutions. But Lucretius is not a utopian. Though the husbands agreed to refrain from harming each others' families (and in the process created the village and its rudimentary civilities), 'it was not possible to achieve perfect unity of purpose'. Complete *concordia* eluded them; they all took the oath, but not everyone kept it. 'Yet a substantial majority kept faith honestly. Otherwise the entire human race would have been wiped out there and then instead of being propagated, generation after generation, down to the present time' (1024-7). 'We must love one another or die.' The verse that Auden violently expunged from his great poem, 'September 1, 1939,' before he

2. *The Gospel of Pleasure*

categorically renounced the poem entire, may be useful here in framing the precision of Lucretius' phrasing (and in impeding any effort to sentimentalise what it represents). Lucretius does not suggest that husbands and fathers should (or could) love one another; but he does insist that an understanding of one's own most personal pleasures (my wife, my children, my hearth, our lives together) may be the bridge to understanding the similar pleasures of others like oneself, and that that understanding might be a beginning of wisdom, that is to say, of a sort of Epicurean *caritas*. That this materialist ethic should depend upon hands warming over a fire, hearing the wind roar outside your hut, the giggles of the marriage bed, and the smiles of meuling and puking infants, will not meet the standards of many serious moralists, but it is Lucretius' version of how a beast became a civilised human being and how morality was born from pleasure in order to engender pleasure and guide it and guard it.

Fire and the city

Necessity and 'practical convenience' (*utilitas*) prompted humans to abandon their 'gestures and inarticulate cries' for the beginnings of human speech and human language. They discovered fire when lightning or the boughs of trees rubbing together chanced to produce it. They learned how to cook food by watching what the heat of the sun did as they walked about the fields. Now the stage is set for another decisive shift in their habits and values:

As time went by, men learnt to change their old way of life by means of fire and other new inventions, instructed by those of outstanding ability and mental energy. Kings began to found cities and establish citadels for their own safeguard and refuge. They parcelled cattle and lands, giving to each according to his looks, his strength, and his ability; for good looks were highly prized and strength counted for much. (1105-11)

We may be tempted to smirk at this emphasis on the role of beauty in the distribution of wealth (until we reflect on the premium our own society puts upon 'looking good'), but probably we won't feel much like laughing when we have noticed the poet's linking of technology and political power. Though he elides the transition from headmanship to bigmanship, he has no trouble in making the connections that obtain among engines for the production of wealth, the power of those who collect and distribute wealth, and their means of protecting it: building the citadel, walling it round, staffing it with soldiers. It is the birth of the city:

> Afterwards came the invention of property and the discovery of gold, which speedily robbed the strong and handsome of their status. The man of greater riches finds no lack of strong frames and comely faces to follow his train. (1113-16)

Here both the brawny and the beautiful have been demoted from their initial high standing by a king who treats everyone as slaves. Cattle and acres yield to gold which is easier to control and to distribute than livestock and land. The effects of this movement from real to unreal (or symbolic) wealth persist to the present day, says Lucretius, who at this moment glides into a riff on the Epicurean simple life. 'Yet if a man would guide his life by true philosophy, he will find ample riches in a modest livelihood enjoyed with a tranquil mind. Of that little he need never be beggared' (1117-18).

This observation smacks, perhaps, of the bromides that clutter Latin literature (and the literatures of not a few other empires, since it is part of the ideology of empire to praise the moral excellence of the good old days that made us what we are today and to wallow in nostalgia for those simpler, more frugal and more virtuous times); but Lucretius, note, doesn't play that card. Others celebrate the humble grandeur of pristine Rome. For Lucretius, the moment fire and power and gold enter into their unholy union the destruction of moral life has begun:

> Men craved for fame and power so that their fortune might rest on a firm foundation and they might live out a peaceful life in the enjoyment of plenty. An idle dream. In struggling to gain the pinnacle of power they beset their own road with perils. (1120-4)

Hoist with their own petard! Peaceful lives and power (along with the fame and fortune that attend them) are a contradiction in terms. What

54

makes a peaceful life possible for an Epicurean is that, for him, enough
= plenty. The pinnacle of power (as we shall soon see, of almost
anything) is not the spacetime for you if a good life is what you have
in mind; it is the place that thunderbolts and envy home in on: 'Far
better to lead a quiet life in subjection than to long for sovereign
authority and lordship over kingdoms' (1129-30). Let those addicted to
power 'sweat blood' to get what they hanker for. All that these people
know (and value and aim at) they have learned from other people
(literally, from an alien mouth), and it is this second-hand knowledge
that maps their desires and their values for them. They do not use
their own eyes and ears to form their own conceptions of what the
world is and what it offers, of what brings happiness and what does
not (as they would do, if atomic truth and the ethics of hedonism that
it promotes had refigured their minds). What they are trying to do
doesn't work, and never has, and never will (1135). At first glance,
these admonitions, too, might be mistaken for hoary moralising. But,
again, their subversion of the Roman Way distinguishes them from
utterances they might seem to resemble. Better to be ruled, to obey,
than to rule others? This is heresy for a Roman, but for an Epicurean
is his catechism in a nutshell. Once you have understood your place
among the atoms and the void, the folly of Roman power flashes clear
as sunlight on your mind. Then you can think for yourself, you need
not remain as you were, a drone in the hive, you can be free – to live a
tranquil, that is to say, a genuine life.

This moment in the story of how humans became human (and
therefore capable of becoming Epicureans) is as crucial as the moment
when beasts became fathers and mothers, husbands and wives. The
earlier moment looks to the house, the domestic space (which may be
seen as Lucretius' version, a Roman version, of Epicurus' garden), a
place where the Epicurean conducts his private life. There is no place
(not the forum, not the army camp, not the houses of rich and powerful,
none of the traditional Roman spaces) where he can conduct his public
life as a Roman Epicurean. All he can do is become an internal émigré.
Because the good life and the Roman life are incompatible, because
equanimity and power (whether you wield it or serve those who wield
it) are a contradiction in terms. From this point on, the story of the
progress of civilisation will continue to unfold (and with it, all but
hidden, the story of the growth of Rome's power), but that story will

also be the story of a journey towards decline and fall: there is an unpersuadable dialectic at work in the processes of material and cultural progress, one in which there is a price (often a moral price) for everything, one in which every solution to every problem tends to create new problems (often moral ones).

Thus, the kings who brought order out of the comparative chaos of scattered hamlets are killed, only to be replaced by mob rule and anarchy. This evil in turn gives way to a rule of law when 'some men showed how to appoint state officials, to establish civil rights and duties so that men would want to obey the laws' (1143-4). Weary of living in violence and discord, mankind 'was the more ready to submit of its own free will to the bondage of laws and institutions' (1146-7). The invention of the republic and the rule of law clearly constitutes a remarkable advance in human affairs. The problem is (we've seen it before with the establishment of family values and of compassion) not everyone (or, not many) are really eager to obey the laws and keep 'the mutual compact of social life' (1155). These people, as the poet drily remarks, find it difficult 'to lead a peaceful and untroubled life' (1154). The rule of law does not make these people better, it does not reform them. For them 'the enjoyment of life's prizes' (for a Roman, these are fame, power and fortune won in the political scramble) is spoiled (1151). In short, they develop bad cases of guilty conscience. But, as Roman History in general and the history of the late Republic in particular make clear, their feelings of guilt do not stop them, ever, from continuing to violate 'the mutual compact of social life'.

The real solution to these difficulties is not, then, the invention or re-invention of republican institutions but the conversion of individuals to the gospel of pleasure and atomistic truth. Lucretius knows that the city's corrupt politicians will not be converted, but if enough of them (see p. 52) were to be converted, that might give Rome (and civilisation) a fighting chance; failing that, the converted can always retreat to their gardens or their hearths (or, later, to their monasteries). The republic was a good idea, it was a big improvement, but it did not work (and it could not work), because, until humans understand and accept the facts of the universe and their place in it, they will continue to be enslaved by false and destructive desires, and they will continue to try to self-medicate their worst sickness (ignorance) with poisonous illusions, the worst of which is that money and power will set everything right (because, rich and powerful or not, everyone is promised a slice of the pie or some of the crumbs: that's how everyone's duped).

The pleasant spectacle of the Republic's power-hungry politicians suffering guilt-induced anxiety attacks triggers in the poet's mind the existence of another sort of mental turbulence. It is time for him to offer a leisurely sketch (1161-240) of the genealogy of organised superstition, whose origins mark another crucial stage in the ascent of the species and its cultural evolution:

> What has implanted in mortal hearts that chill of dread which even now rears new temples of the gods the wide world over and packs them on holy days with pious multitudes? The explanation is not far to seek. Already in those early days men had visions when their minds were awake, and more clearly in sleep, of divine figures, outstanding in beauty and impressive in stature. (1161-8)

Those images were and are real, if misleading. They emanate from the distant gods whom Epicurus revered, as we have seen, for their wisdom and their complete imperturbability. But early men misinterpreted what they saw, even as men do today. They ascribed to the gods qualities they don't have. They confused these conclusions with their perceptions and misconceptions about meteorology. They thought the gods governed storms and earthquakes and volcanoes, and they elaborated this system of error by ascribing vast powers and passions to the gods, whom they therefore tried to appease. Hence the temples and the rituals, the needless anxiety, the proliferation of delusion, the waste of money and of time: all of which persists to the present day. True piety is the invention of Epicurus; it is his vision of the gods as they are, it is his style of prayer: 'to contemplate the universe with a quiet mind', 1203).

> When we gaze up at the supernal regions of this mighty world, at the ether poised above, studded with flashing stars, and there comes into our minds the thought of the sun and moon and their migrations, then in hearts already racked with other woes a new anxiety begins to waken and rear up its head. We fall to

57

wondering whether we may not be subject to some unfathomable power, which speeds the shining stars along with their various tracks. It comes as a shock to our faltering minds to realise how little they know about the world. (1204-11)

'Altogether,' says Santayana, 'at each moment, and in every particular, we are in the hands of some alien, inscrutable power.' This is perhaps the mirror image of the oceanic feeling. This ontological vertigo (what is the world's beginning, what is its end, can time have a stop?) is then personified and worshipped. Once thunder and lightning and storms at sea and earthquakes are added to this figure as its proper mise-en-scène, the result is an overpowering sense of divine omnipotence and human abjection: 'what wonder if mortal men despise themselves and find a place in nature for supernatural forces and miraculous divine powers with supreme control over the universe?' (1238-40).

Welcome to the Iron Age

Having finished his anatomy of superstition, the poet remarks blandly: 'We come next to the discovery of copper, gold and iron, weighty silver and useful lead' (1241-2). Gold? Haven't we learned about gold already (p. 68)? It's been argued that this awkward repetition of gold is a sign of the poem's incomplete state when the poet died. This may be the case, but we can also suppose that Lucretius is less interested in narrative cohesion and tidy sequences than he is in his moral map. In the earlier passage gold (and all it symbolises) was needed when the poet wanted to posit the complicity of money with irresponsible power and irresponsible technology. Here, the mineral is needed to make another point, one that is (again) both once moral and technological.

Humans discovered the existence of useful metals by accident, either when lightning ignited a forest fire, or when men deliberately set fire to the forest in order to scare off rivals they were fighting with or to clear the forest for pasturage or to kill off wild beasts. Lucretius has a fondness for positing multiple hypotheses (this practice helps guard against too easily converting raw sense impressions into inaccurate conceptions, it exercises the learner's powers of imagining and refining images into thoughts, it emphasises that some things are not yet susceptible of being known because we have insufficient evidence). In this instance, there is no way to be sure, hints the poet, of how metals were discovered: 'Let us take it, then, that for one reason or another, no matter what, a fierce conflagration, roaring balefully, has devoured a forest down to the roots and roasted the earth with penetrative fire' (1252-5). Men see the melted veins after they have been solidified into the shapes of the spots where they came to rest, and they begin messing around with them. After some trial and error they begin to think of uses the metals could be put to: weaponry, logging, carpentry. They quickly learn that silver and gold are not well suited to these purposes and, paradoxically, they end up valuing bronze over gold because the edges of a golden implement are soon blunted. But these values are eventually transformed:

> Now it is bronze that is despised, while gold has succeeded to the highest honours. So the circling years bring round reversals of fortune. What once was prized is afterward held cheap. In its place, something else emerges from ignominy, is daily more and more coveted and, as its merits are detected, blossoms into glory, and is acclaimed by mankind with extravagant praises (1274-80).

The blossoming (floret) that marks specific moments of triumph in the technological project ironically underscores what interests the poet most about our kind's genius for and fascination with the making of mechanisms. Our unending technological project is natural to us (natural, like blossoming plants) even though the products (the fruits) of technology come about through a transforming, a denaturing, of natural objects. Yet despite these alterations (natural man transforming nature) the project of technology remains bound by the laws of nature (creation and destruction; the passage from birth through maturation to decline and death): no style of contraption is perdurable. Note that when men begin to value bronze over gold, they do so for purely practical reasons. They have need of certain implements and they choose the metal that better accords with that need. But when they begin to value gold over bronze, their needs become less governed by the criteria of necessity and nature than they had been when, having learned to make their weapons and their tools from iron, their esteem for gold diminished.

A rational mapping of technological progress tends to favor linear ascent and uniform improvement. What the passage before us points to is an alternative, coexisting and contrary pattern, one in which fashion (boredom cured by novelty) could come to count as much as utility. In this pattern, where necessity and nature are overwhelmed by luxury (desires and objects of desire that are neither necessary nor natural), a sort of imitation progress disguises what is in fact regression or digression (to a dead end), one in which our configurations of desires and values (our moral codes) are perverted by a new (and unreal) system of needs and ways of satisfying them.

Lucretius underlines this complex of ironies by addressing Memmius directly when he continues his description of the history of metallurgy:

> At this point, Memmius, you should find it easy to puzzle out for yourself how men discovered the properties of iron. The earliest weapons were hands, nails and teeth. Next came stones and branches wrenched from trees, and fire and flame as soon as these were discovered. Then men learned the use of tough iron and bronze. (1281-6)

It's easy for you, Memmius, because you're a military man who understands good weaponry. Which means: the soldier can quickly see how ridiculous was the notion that swords and spear heads could be made from gold and what a superb breakthrough it was when bronze weapons gave way to iron weapons. Hands and mouths are the weapons we were born with; these we share, unequally, with other beasts. To make up for the poverty of our natural claws and fangs, we had recourse to other (essentially natural) weapons we found lying about: stones and branches. Fires we had to learn to start by rubbing twigs together or striking flint on stone, and that was a technical advance beyond the bestial weapons an ape might use, a rock or a tree trunk. Then came the metals, and with them real, human, rational weapons. Memmius understands that, and he knows, as a philosopher or man in the street might not know (or be willing to remember), how close is weaponry to the heart of technology. Other people, those who haven't served in the army, might reasonably think that the plough or the hammer mattered as much as or more than the sword. Such arguments are valid, but the real truth of the matter is:

> Then men learnt to use tough iron and bronze. Actually the use of bronze was discovered before that of iron, because it was more easily handled and in more plentiful supply. With bronze they tilled the soil. With bronze they whipped up the clashing waves of war, scattered a withering seed of wounds and made a spoil of flocks and fields. Before their armament all else, naked and unarmed, fell an easy prey. Then by slow degrees the iron sword came to the fore, the bronze sickle fell into disrepute, the ploughman began to cleave the earth with iron and on the darkling field of battle the odds were made even. (5.1287-96)

They, our ancestors at the dawn of 'modern' technology, 'tilled the soil' with bronze and cut their harvests with 'the bronze sickle', but it is their bronze (and later their iron) weapons that dominate this passage. In Homer's Shield of Achilles (and in Auden's homage to it), the farmer/soldier//peace/war antinomy is exquisitely balanced; in Lucretius, what he regards as the antinomy's fundamental imbalance is captured with deft irony in (almost) a single verse: *aereque belli / miscebant fluctus et vulnera vasta serebant* (1290). 'With bronze they kept stirring up the tides of war and they kept on sowing' – not seeds but – 'desolate wounds', wounds that make desolate the farmer's fields where battles destroy farmer-soldiers along with their farms ('and made a spoil of flocks and fields'). The new weapons are irresistible. Though farmers do use iron for their ploughs, what caps this section is a final, ironic statement of technological progress: iron produces an even killing field 'in dubious battle, dubious because now equal'. The word that 'darkling' translates, *creper*, is archaic and its feeling-tone is, exactly, 'darkling': 'occurring in darkness, characterised by darkness'. The word's rarity and oddness (not its logical connotation, 'uncertain, obscure') colour the section it closes with something uncanny, sinister.

Intermezzo with tamed savage beasts

The ominous shading at the close of the previous section suffuses what follows it: the poet turns from metallurgy's contributions to the arts of war and looks at what animals can do for the war effort. Without horses neither the cavalry nor war-chariots are possible. (Some chariots are fitted with scythes, and Lucretius describes the damage these can do back in Book 3, where he paints ghastly pictures of wounds that soldiers suffer in battle: 642-56.) It was the Carthaginians who came up with the idea of training elephants to participate in warfare: 'So tragic discords gave birth to one invention after another for the intimidation of the nation's fighting men and added daily increments to the horrors of war', (1305-6). Daily innovations (an interestingly gross exaggeration, at the time it was made) are generated by tragic discord. That seems a rational description of what are (or seem) rational solutions to a perdurable irrational problem. But sometimes the mechanical process (progress) that discord and its necessities have set in motion goes haywire, and the battlefield becomes a nightmare zoo:

Bulls, too, were enlisted in the service of war and the experiment was made of launching savage boars against the enemy. Some even tried an advance guard of doughty lions with armed trainers and harsh masters to discipline them and keep them on the lead. But these experiments failed. The savage brutes, inflamed by promiscuous carnage, spread indiscriminate confusion among the squadrons, as they tossed the terrifying manes on their heads this way and that. The riders failed to soothe the breast of their steeds, panic-stricken by uproar, and to direct them against the enemy. The lionesses hurled their frenzied bodies in a random spring, now leaping full in the face of oncomers, now snatching the unsuspecting victims from behind and dragging them to the ground, mortally wounded in the embrace and gripped by tenacious jaws and crooked claws. The bulls tossed men of their own side and trampled them underfoot and with their horns gored the flanks and bellies of horses from below and hacked up the very earth with minds determined on violence. The infuriated boars with their stout tusks slashed their allies. They reddened with their own blood the weapons broken in their bodies. They mowed down horse and foot pell-mell. (5.1308-29)

This passage continues in the same vein for another ten verses. It reminds me not a little, to use a modern instance, of the bat-bombs – bombs tied to bats – that an Arizona dentist persuaded President Roosevelt to use against the Japanese in World War II (the uncooperative bats blew up one another and various wrong targets).

Commenting on the ancient instances that Lucretius furnishes, C.D.N. Costa remarks on these lines: 'This is probably the most notorious passage in the whole poem. It has baffled generations of commentators, who have been disturbed both by the extent of the macabre and gory detail L. gives us and by our ignorance of the tradition which he is clearly following' (142-3). Costa goes on to inform his readers that Lucretius may be following a lost tradition concerning beasts-in-human-war that is faintly visible when other writers mention oxen, dogs and camels as living weapons, and that validates the suggestion that some of the poet's inspiration may have come from 'the horrors of the popular wild beast shows with which he would have been all too familiar'. But what matters rhetorically are the strenuous hyperbole of the imagery and the pattern that is formed when the poet keeps pointing out that the animals turn on their trainers, their fellow soldiers, *many* of them (1323, 1326, 1340). The passage is not only 'notorious,' it is also powerful and effective *as poetry*. It easily rivals similar passages in Vergil, in Ovid, and in Lucan (gorily purple patches crammed with surreal wounds). It sounds like superb (if archaic) epic poetry. The pictures are vivid and neatly crafted. Sound and sight flawlessly combine to produce poetic satisfaction. Why go to all this trouble to promote a minor 'tradition' of failed (and absurd) military technology, one that the poet himself instantly rejects? 'If, indeed,' he blandly concludes, 'the experiment was ever tried. For my part, I find it hard to believe that men had no mental apprehension and premonition of this mutual disaster and disgrace before it could happen' (1341-3). If it was so hard to believe, why waste a page of gorgeous verse on it? Or, if he just couldn't resist the urge to try his hand at this scene of slaughter, why not toss it into the wastebasket after he'd had his fun, thus saving the integrity of his poem?

Though I can hardly insist that the passage in question cannot represent a mistaken experiment that the poet would have excised had he lived to revise his poem, I can suggest that those who are displeased with the passage may be taking it too seriously (and therefore, not seriously enough). As Lucretius represents them, bulls, boars, and lions are all reluctant and unreliable participants in a single battle. There were 'experiments', we're told, yet here they have all been conflated into what appears to be one hair-raising, widescreen engagement in stereophonic sound. This passage, I suggest, is a satirist's cartoon version of the technological imperative in its martial mode. You would think that these military engineers (like the Arizona dentist) might have considered the possibility that what they were doing could end in 'mutual disaster and disgrace'. If you thought that, you'd be wrong: because the technological imperative abhors any limit to its imagination. The poet drily admits that the historical tradition for animal warriors (except for horses and elephants) is to be rejected (Kenney 350). 'It would be safer to assert that this has happened somewhere in the universe, somewhere in the multiplicity of diversely formed worlds, than in any one specific globe' (1344-6). The invention of Bestial Special Forces, then, is something that happens on Mars, it is Plan 9 From Outer Space. It is something so absurd that no rational human being could entertain it for a second. Or, if it is not something that happened long ago in another galaxy, it could only 'have been undertaken more to spite the enemy than with any hope of victory, by men mistrustful of their own numbers and armaments, but not afraid to die', (1347-9). A strategy of revenge or of despair. Something crazy, something beyond reason or analysis.

Here, the technological imperative is wittily taken to its illogical conclusion. Making weapons (as well as ploughshares and looms) is not in itself a stupid idea, but all technological inventions, like the desires for the increase of pleasure and the decrease of pain that inspire those inventions, must be made to subject themselves to an exact ethical scrutiny, one where the limits of technology and the limits of pleasure are precisely linked and precisely drawn. In the cartoon, as occasionally in life, the lunatic inventors (or their masters) are out of control (Saylor 314-16).

2. The Gospel of Pleasure

A decent living

We expect that the poet will now return to the main line of his story: the tale of our kind's triumphal struggle for civilisation (in which this peculiar shaggy beast story was no more than an inexplicable detour). Such a resumption would doubtless cause us to forget that his serious representation of the progress of military technology had lurched its way into ghoulish laughter. And resume his tale he does. He takes up the topic of costume ('plaited clothes came before woven ones', because for weaving you need looms and for looms you need iron, 1350-1). Nature, intervening once again in the process of culture, gendered weaving as male rather than as female because men are brighter and more artistic than women. But weaving looked like women's work to tough farmers, so, rather than be thought effete by them, virile weavers left weaving to the women and returned to the great outdoors and its backbreaking toil. The next section follows the weavers back to the farm and concerns itself with the sowing and grafting of plants and experiments in cultivation. The farmers

> tried one type of cultivation after another in their treasured plot. They saw the wild fruits grow mild in the ground with cosseting and humouring. Day by day they kept forcing the woodland to creep further up the hillside, surrendering the lower reaches to tillage. Over hill and plain, they extended meadowland, reservoirs, watercourses, cornland and laughing vineyards, with the distinctive grey-green olives running between, rippling over hump and hollow and along the level ground. So their countryside assumed its present aspect of varied beauty, interspersed with luscious orchards and marked out by encircling hedges of luxuriant trees. (1361-78)

This is the technology of Epicurean Arcadia, the unity of nature and machine, the fusion of leaf and iron, in an Italian paradise. The 'encircling hedges of luxuriant trees' create something like Epicurus' garden inside a wider garden – the Italian landscape that men with tools have sweated hard (pain for the sake of pleasure and need) to bring slowly into existence. Here the orthodox Epicurean distinction between pleasures that are necessary and pleasures that are natural seems to disappear. If there is some small difference here between what is necessary and what is natural, there is certainly nothing in this picture that is unnecessary or unnatural. The implements of farming (there is no mention of iron) are invisible here, and by now we may have forgotten the intrusive phantasmagoria of bestial slaughter (and the martial technophiles and their murderous lunacies) along with war itself. The poet has engineered a final transformation, it seems, and civilisation has become truly civil, truly a spacetime for the gospel of pleasure and the atomic truth that fosters it. Here Nature is not so much tamed as it is enhanced; these men don't dominate the landscape, they live in it, decently. They, like their lands, are at once natural and cultivated. Their effort to minimise their suffering by working to secure the enjoyment of things necessary and natural has civilised them (and their land) without transforming them into cosmopolitan sybarites.

When they aren't labouring in the fields and vineyards and orchards, men learn the rudiments of music: '... by slow degrees, they learnt those plaintive melodies that flow from the flute ... in the solitudes where the shepherd spends his sunlit leisure. These are the tunes that soothed and cheered their hearts after a full meal' (1384-7; 1390-1). A lunch break, a full belly, music: are these necessary? The lunch break, yes, but this may be rather a protracted one. The full belly might portend indigestion, hence pain, hence an Epicurean lapse. Music? Certainly not necessary and not really natural. Or is it? It was learned from nature, after all, and it answers a need (one that is possibly universal?). 'Soothed and cheered their hearts.' This is a pleasure that will not entail pain (and probably the full belly won't either). It delights the ear and the spirit, it helps these men relax, it enhances their respite and thus helps define the rhythm of their work day. It is not perhaps necessary (but perhaps it is), it is certainly natural. Furthermore, it helps unite them. This is, as it happens, a picnic, Italian style:

So they would often recline in company on the soft grass by a running stream under the branches of a tall tree and refresh their bodies pleasurably at small expense. Better still if the sun smiled upon them and the season of the year emblazoned the green herbage with flowers. Then was the time for joking and

66

talking and merry laughter. Then was the heyday of the rustic
muse. Then light-hearted jollity prompted them to wreathe head
and shoulders with garlands twisted of flowers and leaves and to
dance out of step, moving their limbs clumsily and with clumsy
foot stamping on mother earth. This was matter enough for mirth
and boisterous laughter. For these arts were still in their youth,
with all the charm of novelty. (1392-404)

Food, music, sunlight – but, above all, fellowship. As I've said before,
Lucretius says precious little about friendship, which is central to
Epicurus' scheme, but here we come upon a charming snapshot of
friends together at play. From the perspective offered here (Epicurean
with more than a dash of Italy) conviviality is both natural and
necessary, it is an essential part of living decently. If being without
pain were all there is to life, one could live, like a pagan monk, in a
closed garden or a cell, contemplating truth, enjoying one's own imperturbability. But Lucretius' final image in his history of civilisation is of
ordinary people living the decent, Epicurean life unawares, and, then
suddenly, bursting into a wild celebration of their well-being. In the
full rush of their enthusiasm they invent something like the carnival
(the poet disguises the fact that their behaviour makes most sense if
they have gathered together on a holy day) and then they invent the
dance. Perhaps they dance in honour of the mother earth they dance
upon. Or perhaps this is a sort of Epicurean holy day in honour of
Nature, not as a providential divinity but as a mysterious, omnipotent
process, which of course is what she is in the poem's great opening
section. As another hedonist poet puts it:

> Supple and turbulent, a ring of men
> Shall chant in orgy on a summer morn
> Their boisterous devotion to the sun,
> Not as a god, but as a god might be,
> Naked among them like a savage source.

It is here, in the epiphany of Nature as Pleasure, that Lucretius places
the acme of the ascent of our species toward its good. In most other
humanist versions of human progress, it is the metropolis and its
riches, its arts and laws and learning, that make up the pinnacle of

67

human achievement. Lucretius has dealt with these already. They are, paradoxically speaking, not so much necessary as inevitable; they are, or become, unnatural. Without the light of Epicurus to cleanse them, they are corrupted and corrupting, for they tend (such is the power of irrational and traditional ideologies over collective opinion) to distort our concepts of what is necessary and natural. Like beasts, our first ancestors could not do much to escape from pain before they began their ascent to civilisation; but the denizens of the metropolis, masters of the civilised life, are over-ripe and cannot readily distinguish true pleasures from the fake pleasures they use to hide from pains both real and imaginary. It is in his picture of an ordinary picnic where friends are eating, singing, joking, laughing, dancing, that the poet gives us our best glimpse of humans who, no longer beasts and not yet spoiled hedonists, are capable of true pleasure.

True pleasure

The art of music has evolved since its primitive origins, and that development is both natural and laudable. That evolution, however, doesn't mean that modern musicians get any more fun out of their sophisticated artistry than did 'the woodland race sprung from the soil' (1411).

> What we have here and now, unless we have known something more pleasing in the past, gives the greatest satisfaction and is reckoned the best of its kind. Afterwards the discovery of something new and better blunts and vitiates our enjoyment of the old. So we have lost our taste for acorns. So we have abandoned those couches littered with herbage and heaped with leaves. So the wearing of wild beasts' skins has gone out of fashion. (1412-18)

We moderns have made abundant progress, no question of that. Fashion is fuelled by the arrival of something new, but it is not mere novelty that drives fashion, it is also the desire for improvement that makes us turn from what is old towards what is new. For instance, we no longer subsist on acorns or sleep on the ground or wear animal hides.

So much the poet grants to material progress. Then he lets us have it between the eyes:

And yet I daresay that the invention of this costume provoked such envy that its first wearer met his death in an ambush and the costume itself was so daubed with blood and torn to shreds by rival claimants that it could not be used by anyone. Skins yesterday, purple and gold today – such are the baubles that embitter human life with resentment and waste it with war. (1419-24)

The first skin garment, a giant step towards comfort and civilisation, already spelled trouble. In its bloody state, after it was snatched from the corpse of its proud inventor, it became the cause of a bloody skirmish which prefigured bigger wars when the inventions and the prizes got larger. Primitive luxuries or today's outrageous luxuries, all are baubles – if they 'embitter human life with resentment and waste it with war'. But the poet is not in doubt as to where to lay the real blame: 'In this I do not doubt that the greater blame rests with us' (1425). He rethinks what he's just said. That fatal skin garment was not really a bauble (he had yielded for a moment to a satirist's easiest temptation, useless hyperbole): 'To the earth-born generation in their naked state the lack of skins meant real discomfort; but we suffer no distress by going about without robes of purple, brocaded with gold and extravagant figures, so long as we have some plebeian wrap to throw around us (1426-9).

Our ancestors were fighting off real pain. We are fighting off imaginary pains with pleasures that are neither necessary nor natural (call them unreal pleasures). We live ugly stupid lives in a world of illusions, we live, in the words of Michael Harrington, in 'the desolation of empty abundance'. Lucretius is ruthless in his condemnation: 'So mankind is perpetually the victim of a pointless and futile martyrdom, fretting life away in fruitless worries through failure to realise what limit is set to acquisition and to the growth of genuine pleasure' (1430-44).

This is not the voice of one of Rousseau's dimmer epigones, nor that of a radical-chic Luddite, inveighing against phallocratic science. Lucretius knows perfectly well that there is good technology and bad technology (he would not recognise the notion of neutral technology). He knows that we humans are technological animals, he knows that natural necessities impel us to find ways of losing pain and finding pleasure. But he also knows that unless the pursuit of pleasure is illumined by the wisdom of Epicurus, we will constantly lose sight of true pleasure and will constantly arrange our priorities in the wrong order. (A contemporary instance that has just come to my attention: 'Millions for Viagra, Pennies for Diseases of the Poor', title of an essay on the cover of *The Nation*, 19 July 1999.) It is this misrecognition of our real needs and their proper orderings that taints our perceptions and corrupts our souls with its misimaginings.

That habit of misrecognition can be changed; we can freely learn to unlearn the dreadful errors that corrupt culture and our own anxieties impose on us. It is because we are free to change that, unless we change, the fault is ours (Mitsis 147-51; see also pp. 20, 29). Our natural desire for progress has propelled our movement toward moral and material culture, but our perverted desire for fake progress (one in which material progress fails to engender moral progress, one in which we forget how to distinguish good from bad technology) 'has driven life steadily onward, out to the high seas, and has stirred up from the depths the surging tides of war' (1434-5). The echoes of the fight over the skin garment, and, more powerfully, of lines 1289-96 above (the coming of iron weapons) furnish the poet's tale of our progress with its real conclusion.

The heart of civilization is technology and the heart of technology are the weapons that corrupt desire and cause it to take more than it needs, to take what it doesn't need, to destroy whatever stands in its way. Societies are organised around this corruption and the machines it uses to try to satisfy itself. In this sense, society as it exists is essentially evil. Societies need not be evil, but until their citizens learn true pleasure they will remain so.

That clinches it, but the satirist cannot resist an ironic coda. He points out that astronomers, studying the sun and the moon, 'taught men that the seasons of the year revolve and that there is a constant pattern in things and a constant sequence' (1438-9). Even before the astronomers informed men about what happened in heaven people had built fortifications and parcelled out the land (we have heard this before). 'The deep sea flowered with sail-flying ships. Societies were bound together by compacts and alliances.' Yes, yes, we know that. 'Poets were beginning to record history in song.' That *is* a new addition to the tale of how civilisation grew. But the poet unfortunately defabricates the meaning of his statement by reminding us that these poets started their task just as literacy was beginning, so 'our age cannot look back to see what happened before this stage, except in so far as its traces can be uncovered by reason' (1446-7). That is to say, we have to make inferences about the story he's been telling us, we have to guess. We have, more or less, to make it up. Then his final conclusion:

> So we find not only such arts as seafaring and agriculture, city walls and laws, weapons, roads and clothing [that skin garment again], but also without exception the amenities and refinements of life, poetry, pictures and statues, artfully carved and polished, all were taught gradually by usage and the active mind's experiments as men groped their way forward step by step. So each particular development is brought gradually to the fore by the advance of time, and reason lifts it into the light of day. Men saw one notion after another take shape within their minds until by their arts they scaled the topmost peak, *ad summum cacumen*. (1448-57)

Costa's judgment on 1440-57 is as follows: 'This final section of the book is both a resumé of some of man's progress which has already been discussed and a summary catalogue of further advances. These include literature and other arts of cultivated life, which appropriately mark the climax of man's civilised achievements in the last line of the book. However, it can be argued that these last paragraphs are not as highly wrought as one might expect in a conclusion, and there are some grounds for thinking that the passage on music ... was the original, or at least an alternative, ending' (152). Indeed, 'not highly wrought' at all, in fact rather casual, verging on the slipshod. What matters here is the final, fatal phrase, 'the topmost peak'. 'In struggling to obtain the *pinnacle* of power they beset their own roads with perils. And then from the very *peak*, as though by a thunderbolt, they are cast down by envy ...' (1123-5); 'Now it is bronze that is despised, while gold has succeeded to the highest honours. So the circling years bring round reversals of fortune' (1275-6). (The same notion of the dangerous eminence of completion recurs: 2.1116ff., 2.1130, 5.1141; see also 2.13 and 3.63.) The top is a dangerous place and an ephemeral place. Perhaps it would have been better to stay at the picnic than go

71

out and conquer first one's Italian neighbours, then the world. Poetry and the fine arts are all very well, but, delightful though they are, they are too often implicated in the configuration of values and desires that engender and are engendered by a corrupt society, one in which entertainment is transformed into ideology, and ideology, into entertainment. The only real diversion, the only real refuge, the only real civilisation, is the one that Epicurus has revealed to us. Without him, ordinary civilisations are a snare and a delusion.

A last glimpse of the worst

The link between the close of Book 5 and the beginning of Book 6 could hardly be firmer: 'In days of old it was from Athens of high renown that the knowledge of cereal crops was first disseminated among suffering mankind. It was Athens that built life on a new plan and promulgated laws ...' (1-3). Athens gave the Western world more than that, and it was already, in the poet's time, what it would become again in the Renaissance, with the revival of Greek studies in the West: the womb of humanism and the paragon of civilisation. It gave suffering humanity its best source of food, it renewed life, and provided it with law and order. Well and good. But the sentence continues, taking a different turn:

It was Athens no less that first gave to life a message of good cheer through the birth of that man, gifted with no ordinary mind, whose unerring lips gave utterance to the whole truth. Even now, when he is no more, the widespread and long-established fame of his divine discoveries is exalted to the very skies. (4-8)

Athens is the best of cities, its claims to fame are imposing: it reduced human suffering and enriched human life. But superb though its contributions to mankind were, they are, in comparison with those of Epicurus, its greatest alumnus, liable to the objections that the poet has just finished raising in the ironic peroration to his history of human progress. Although Athens gave humans things they really needed and a new life livable under new laws, it made its most distinctive constribution to minimising human suffering when it produced Epicurus.

This saviour of mortals was himself mortal, but his discoveries were superhuman (*divina*). Athens itself is, in the poet's day, a sleepy college town that tourists like to visit but whose fame has outlived its greatness. The poet is all but immune to the fevers of Romantic Hellenism in its Roman version. For him, cities, like men, are mortal. They wax and wane, they have their vogue, they wither and vanish. He ironically salutes Athens for its most shining claim to fame: he was the son of Athenian parents. Athens, like the poet and his poem, will be destroyed. What endures (as long as his texts endure, as long as literate humans and their planet survive) is the truth of Epicurus. Learning to rejoice in that truth will not rescue us from death, but it can make us look directly at the meaning and limits of our mortality, and when we see that truth we will be free and able to live our portion of spacetime decently, in the light of pleasure's gospel.

What opens Book 6 ends it. Lucretius closes his poem with a picture of the plague at Athens, one copied from Thucydides' account of it. That the poet did not live to complete his poem is (again) possible; it is also possible that the final page of Book 6 (and of the poem) got lost (an easy kind of loss) as the *DRN* was transmitted down through the centuries. I tend to think there may have been a page or so before that loss, not one in which he gave us one last pep talk and admonished us to be cheerful and virtuous, no matter what; rather it would likely have been something formal, something laconic, unobtrusive, generically suitable; it may have been a final hymn of thanksgiving to or about Epicurus. But the fact remains: even if there was some formulaic *envoi*, the end of the poem consists of a horrific portrait of a human community being violently dissolved.

Is that any way to clinch your argument and make converts? No, if what you're after is rhetorical decorum or religious assent. Yes, if what concerns the poet is the quality of the emotional and intellectual transformation of his dialogic partner: he wants to know if we really believe we can look steadily at our worst fears (Fowler 135-8). Memmius and the other skin-deep hedonists that Cicero was so worried might be corrupted by the gospel of pleasure have long since fled, from boredom or dullness or dismay. We're still here, listening. But where is here? Here is, that favourite Lucretian place, on the edge.

Pursuant to his earlier discussions of meteorological phenomena in Book 6, the poet begins (quietly) speculating on the causes of diseases (they are very definitely not punishments sent by gods, Godwin 1991, 169) 'and the source from which the sickly power of pestilence is able to breathe a sudden death-dealing plague upon the tribes of men and herds of beasts' (1090-3). He has already shown (769-80) that there are seeds (atoms) of many things that we need and that 'on the other hand, there must be others flying about that are a cause of disease and death' (1095-6). These lethal atoms (unobservable but inferable) somehow cluster together sometimes and when they do they 'upset the balance of the atmosphere' and 'the air becomes infected' (1096-7). When 'some atmosphere that chances to be uncongenial to us is set in motion, the baleful air begins to creep. Like mist and cloud it glides and, wherever it comes, it sows and disorder and change', and 'when it at length makes its way into our region, it contaminates the atmosphere there, making it comfortable to itself and unfriendly to us' (1119-24). That's what happened when seeds of disease came airborne from Egypt, bringing Athens its famous plague.

When the poet's Greek model, Thucydides, describes that plague, he combines clinical observations of the sickness with sympathetic if restrained depictions of how people reacted to their personal and public disaster. He ends his description of the plague by remarking that some people availed themselves of the city's confusion and general hopelessness to eat, drink and be merry with a vengeance. These Athenians became late-blooming super-hedonists, desperate to grab any and every last pleasure they could (*The Peloponnesian War* 2.53). The Greek historian, then, sums up his representation of his city's agony with an ironic understatement about a breakdown of personal morality that echoes the breakdown of the polity. But the Latin poet, having selected details that evoke the hysteria and the despair the plague induces in everyone, having created an impressionistic canvas on which irrational feelings overwhelm every other concern (Commager 108-14), concludes his depiction of the plague and the poem this way:

> The mode of burial that had hitherto always been in vogue was no longer practised in the city. The whole nation was beside itself with terror. Each in turn, when he suffered bereavement, put

away his own dead hastily, as time allowed. Many unpleasant expedients were inspired by poverty and the suddenness of the event. Men would fling blood-relatives amid violent outcry on the pyres built for others and set torches under them. Often they shed much blood in these disputes rather than abandon their dead. (6.1278-86)

Thucydides had discussed the chaos of funerals during the plague and noted that people made use of the pyres intended for other people's dead to burn their own. But Lucretius' last sentence is his own invention, his own emphasis. The bestialised citizens stage bloody fights over the pyres, as their primitive ancestors had fought over the first skin garment. Civilisation (this is no longer merely the Athens of Pericles or Thucydides, it is every city) has sunk back, horrifically, into the discord which it had (barely) struggled out of. There are some evils the City cannot protect us against, and the City itself may be destroyed by monstrous evils that the truths of classical humanism (Plato, Cicero, the Stoics) are as powerless against as the illusions of religion. And Epicurus, can he protect us when the plague comes?

If we have listened to his warnings and fled (if only in our minds) from the ruining Metropolis, we may escape the spiritual death that this polysymbolic plague threatens us with. But from real death, the plague death, *that* Epicurus cannot save us from; that death is part of the atomic truth ('good' atoms / 'bad' atoms; Creation / Destruction). Nor can he protect us from the extraordinary terrors of extraordinary deaths. If pains (including those of deathbeds) are fierce, he tells us, they are usually brief; if they are long, they are usually mild and endurable. But if they are airborne? If they are sudden and terrifying? If they are violent and, as with the plague, prolonged? If they arrive via earthquake, hurricane, avalanche, flood, volcano, famine, really nasty barbarians at the gates, plagues or: from 'The Demon in the Freezer: How Smallpox, a Disease Officially Eradicated Twenty Years Ago, Became the Biggest Bioterrorist Threat We Now Face' (*New Yorker*, Richard Preston, 12 July 1999)?

No, no: the truth of Epicurus cannot save us – nothing can – from the truth of our mortality. But if we can learn to ponder that truth, in its most dreadful aspect (no gentle deathbeds here, no comfort from grieving friends, no last goodbyes – just 'hostile' atoms tearing us to pieces), then we may have really heard what Epicurus and his Roman poet were really saying to us. Atomic truth and the gospel of pleasure may help us to acquire (some) serenity (as much as we can get); but we are not, like the Stoics, 'toreadors of virtue', and our style of serenity will not protect us against all evils. Note that at 6.33-4, the poet says that Epicurus 'made it clear that, *more often than not*, it was quite needlessly that mankind stirred up stormy waves of disquietude within their breasts' ('more often than not', *plerumque*: the italics are mine). When the hurricane whirls Epicurus up and away, he will feel no more serene than would a Platonist or a Stoic.

But truth, pleasure and serenity can and do combine to cleanse our minds of illusions about who we are and what happens in our world, they instruct us to worry only about evils we can remedy and to spend the time we have thus saved (the little, wonderful, priceless time) on the pleasures of reality. They set us free from ordinary fears and they teach us to avoid unnecessary pain for the enjoyment of true pleasure.

PART II

Our Lucretius

3

A Genealogy of Melancholy

Everywhere you flee God's footprints, but you cannot scuff them
out – it is you they follow, you!   Cardinal Polignac

Lucretius Redux

I won't flatter myself. If I'd been a Christian in the early, middle or late
Middle Ages and worked in a scriptorium and stumbled on a rare copy
of the *DRN*, I'm pretty sure I would instantly have handed it over to
the head monk, suggesting that it be tossed forthwith into the flames
or be whited over and piously reused for making copies of the lives of
various foolish yet saintly virgins. The poem was not wildly popular in
late antiquity, and in Christian times, before the Renaissance, it was,
along with Catullus, almost lost (Hadzsits 160-274). It did not speak
to those Christians, or rather, most of what it had to say to them, when
it was not merely blasphemous, must have sounded all but absurd.
That it had clearly, on the surface of its verse, enormous beauty and
power probably made matters only worse.

And when, in the early Renaissance, it began to be rediscovered,
there were no sudden epiphanies (Hadzsits 248-83). The new scholars
did not look up amazed as they closed their newly found texts of the
DRN and then spill out into the streets from their studies, yelling the
glad tidings of a world without God and without plan or purpose. They
had no trouble finding the beauty and the power of the poetry, and they
were struck with the earnestness of poet's moral rhetoric. But his
theological and philosophical opinions were irrelevant to the humanist
project, and these they set aside for theologians and philosophers to
quarrel over, to champion or anathematise as they wished (Bollack
118-21).

This prudent compartmentalisation, less craven than cagey, set the
stage both for Lucretius' successful entry into the high Western canon

and for the mechanisms that would, down to our own time, ensure the permanence of that success. Humanists (schoolmasters, literary critics, philologists, literary theorists, cultural critics – whatever professors of rhetoric happen to be calling themselves at any given time) are interested in the aesthetic and ethical values that are contained in the texts they preserve and pass on: in Lucretius these values are abundant. The chief difficulties that humanists have in preserving Lucretius and passing him on come about when theologians or philosophers or scientists decide, for various reasons, to open the locked compartment. These meddlers disdain questions of beauty and goodness, and, obsessed with notions of truth, they tend, whenever Lucretius attracts their attention, to pervert the poet's meanings for their own purposes and to endanger his place in the canon by making him dangerous to the dominant sign-system.

The real troubles of the humanistic Lucretius begin with the efforts of the French philosopher and scientist, Pierre Gassendi (1592-1655), to use the poet's poem to explain the doctrines of Epicurus to a world that was just beginning (Galileo was among Gassendi's friends) to invent modern science. Whatever his motives, whatever his kind and degree of faith in the Christian God, Gassendi's achievement was a version of Epicurus for modern (that is, post-medieval) times, a version in which the truth of antique materialism and the truth of the Christian God are made to seem not incompatible (Joy 15-18, 69-70). Since Lucretius provides much of the 'evidence' for what we know about Epicureanism, Gassendi quotes him extensively (Jones 177), thereby conscripting him into the army that would be fighting in the war against Aristotle and Scholasticism until Voltaire picked up his pen and the war was over and the Gothic ghosts were routed.

If Gassendi had not begun using our poet in this fashion, others inevitably would have. However archaic his science, however droll his observations about nature must increasingly have come to seem in the eyes of early-modern scientists, the poet of atomic truth was destined to play a prominent role in the battle between Christian and post-Christian paradigms. The problem for Lucretius (that is, for his humanistic explainers) was: when he became one of Gassendi's best sources for Epicurean doctrine, he became less than the sum of the five thousand (plus) verses that Gassendi quoted in his explication of Epicurus. The style of Lucretian citation that Gassendi ushered in

80

jeopardises the unity of the poem's design and makes its fragmentation the normal way of reading it (for Montaigne's different yet similar habits of Lucretian citation, Jones 160; Hadzsits 272-4). Thus truncated, reduced to footnotes, transformed into evidence and 'authority', the poem became a pawn in the ferocious struggles that would remake religion and science during the next few centuries, then gradually devolved into purple patches and a quarry for historians of ancient Western philosophy.

In 1685, John Dryden published his translations of five passages of Lucretius; twelve years later he would publish a translation of all of Vergil. Perhaps it was because he had this mammoth task already in mind that he decided to english so little of so important a Latin poet and one so suited to his gifts. Or perhaps he decided against translating the whole poem because Thomas Creech, having published a translation of the entire poem only three years before, had stolen his thunder. If that's the case, his bow to Creech is studiously respectful as he acknowledges the debt he owes 'to the ingenious and learned translator of Lucretius' (Preface to *Poems Included in Sylvae*). Then he continues: 'I have not here design'd to rob him of any part of that commendation which he has so justly acquir'd by the whole author, whose fragments only fall to my portion.' He then compares his own mode of translation with Creech's: 'He follows him more closely than I have done, which became an interpreter of the whole poem: I take more liberty, because it best suited my design, which was to make him as pleasing as I could. He had been too voluminous, had he used my method in so long a work; and I had certainly taken his, had I made it my business to translate the whole.' Dryden's purpose, then, is poetic beauty and the pleasures it affords, whereas Creech's was totality and accuracy. It's not clear from what he says that Dryden is telling us everything that might interest us about his decision to render only a few passages from the poem, nor does he quite explain what governed his selection of those passages: Book 1 (1-40), the opening of Book 2 (1-61), from the close of Book 3 (830-1090), from the close of Book 4 (1052-287), and a passage from Book 5 (221-34).

It so happens that the passages Dryden chose from Books 2 and 3 were Gassendi's favourites (Fleischmann 1964, 218; for Gassendi's reception in England, see Joy 13-15;). These are passages which, Dryden says, 'are strong enough to a reasonable man, to make him less in love with life, and consequently in less apprehension of death.' That is to say, they are parts of the poem that can easily find entrance into the sign systems of Christian humanism in its early modern phase and of 'latitudinarian Christian morality' (Fleischmann 1963, 637).

In this version of Christianity and Classical Culture Lucretius can safely shine, with a carefully screened light; like Cicero, Seneca, Plato, Aristotle, Vergil, and the other virtuous pagans, he can be studied without risk of contamination to the reader. To these noble humanist passages Dryden adds the ornate, easily baroque splendour of sexy Venus, fuelling the earth's abundance with her energies and luring Mars from his duties into softporn dalliance ('Sucks in with open lips thy balmy breath,/ By turns restor'd to life, and plung'd in pleasing death); but he was also interested (as usual) in the patriotic bang he could effect:

> There while thy curling limbs about him move,
> Involv'd and fetter'd in the links of love,
> When, wishing all, he nothing can deny,
> Thy charms in that auspicious moment try;
> With willing eloquence our peace implore,
> And quiet to the weary world restore.

Lucretius (who had not mentioned the links of love and their involved fetters) goes on to say: 'In this evil hour of my country's history, I cannot pursue my task with a mind at ease ....' But Dryden had, of course, no reason to end on this somber note and he ends his poem (this fragment) by extracting serene grandeur from exquisite tumult. The passage from Book 4 causes him some concern since he knows that his enemies will censure him for putting into English 'the obscenity of the subject, which is aggravated by the too lively and alluring delicacy of the verses'. He admits the passage pleases him (and he knows it will delight his audience), but he also claims that the passage is instructive: 'I am not so secure from that passion, but that I want my author's antidotes against it. He has given the truest and most philosophical account both of the disease and its remedy, which I ever found in any author: for which reasons I translated him.' And translated him, too, into 'gorgeous English' which never 'minced his meaning, which I am satisfied was honest and instructive'. To do otherwise, would have been to betray his author. To rescue his contemporaries, then, from the ravages of lust (and, at the same time, give them a little of what they fancy), he provides them with the unadulterated poet who must elsewhere be (theologically speaking) bowdlerised or left untranslated.

For his final selection, another fragment that he makes into a poem of his own, Dryden goes to a passage in Book 5 where Lucretius is discussing reality's indifference to humankind: 'the universe was certainly not created for us by divine power, it is so full of imperfections' (198-9). He goes on to explain, through a series of images, that without human toil and human technology, the species could not survive on this planet. When a baby comes screaming his way from the womb into the world ('quite rightly, considering what evils life holds in store for him', 226-7), unlike the beasts, whom Nature provides with their wants, he would perish – without the ingenuity and effort of adult human beings who save him. Nature is 'a clever inventor', who helps beasts, man (imitating nature) is a clever inventor who helps himself. What the passage finally means, in the context of the whole poem, is that, despite human ingenuity, human life is still filled with countless sufferings, sufferings that only a striving individual, after he has been shaped by the teachings of Epicurus and his gospel of pleasure, can mitigate (but not entirely abolish). Obviously, Dryden was not interested in hearing (and he knew *his* audience – whatever Creech's audience might put up with – absolutely would not tolerate hearing) that 'the universe was certainly not created for us by divine power', that God took no interest in us. So, in the poem that Dryden fashions from the lines in question, 'like a sailor by the tempest hurl'd/ Ashore, the babe is shipwrack'd on the world', and, now become a symbol of humankind, of a humankind without God's mercy, he is

> Expos'd upon unhospitable earth,
> From the first moment of his hapless birth,
> Straight with foreboding cries he fills the room;
> Too true presages of his future doom.

A prelapsarian (pagan) nature cares for the (unfallen) beasts, but the guilty, 'shipwrack'd' babe' (a godless Epicurean?) is consigned to the hopelessness of his 'future doom', to pain in this life, to eternal pain in the next. So much for atomic truth and the gospel of pleasure.

If I am not mistaken, the distinguishing character of Lucretius (I
mean of his soul and genius) is a certain kind of noble pride, and
positive assertion of his opinions. He is everywhere confident of
his own reason, and assuming an absolute command, not only
over his vulgar reader, but even his patron Memmius. For he is
always bidding him attend, as if he had a rod over him, and using
a magisterial authority, while he instructs him.

Dryden, a great poet, has read the entire poem, and read it greatly. He
understands exactly who its poet is and how his poem works (his low,
ironic bow to his own aristocratic readers does not mean he has
misread Memmius). But that poem is not one he wants to get identi-
fied with. Lucretius is possessed of a sublime and daring genius whose
thoughts are 'masculine, full of argumentation, and that sufficiently
warm', he has a 'fiery temper' from which 'proceeds the loftiness of his
expressions, and the perpetual torrent of his verse, where the barren-
ness of his subject does not too much constrain the quickness of his
fancy'. But all that superb genius and unfailing power, all that flair for
virile debate (of which Dryden is both possessor and connoisseur),
were essentially wasted: 'For there is no doubt to be made that he
could have been everywhere as poetical as he is in his descriptions and
in the moral part of his philosophy, if he had not aim'd more to instruct
in his *System of Nature*, than to delight. But he was bent upon making
Memmius a materialist, and teaching him to defy an invisible power.
In short, he was so much the atheist, that he forgot sometimes to be a
poet.' (Slightly over a century later, Shelley, agog with Platonic rapture
and transcendental yearnings, would echo this judgment in *A Defense
of Poetry*: 'Lucretius ... limed the wings of his swift spirit in the dregs
of the sensible world'.) Fortunately, having excluded the (many) didactic (and blasphemous) passages (most of the poem), Dryden can con-
trive to fashion a bright bouquet from the remaining poetical passages
and to concentrate his efforts as translator on the 'descriptions and the
moral part of his philosophy'.

   'These are the considerations which I had of that author, before I
attempted to translate *some parts of him*.' Having forced himself to lay
aside his 'natural diffidence and scepticism for a while, to take up that
dogmatical way of his, which ... is so much his character as to make
him that individual poet', Dryden is almost ready to construct his

84

elegant anthology from what is left of the dangerous poem. But he still needs to explain what is absent from his selection (and what some readers may feel as the presence of an absence). 'As for his opinions concerning the mortality of the soul, they are so absurd, that I cannot, if I would, believe them. I think a future state demonstrable even by natural arguments ...'. If you take away the punishments of the afterlife, he continues, people are going to behave very badly here below. He riffs on this for a while, then sums up his final thoughts on Lucretius' dogmatic materialism this way: 'These are my thoughts, abstractly, and without entr'ing into the notions of our Christian faith, which is the proper business of divines.' A recent biographer thinks this short shrift with theology suspect: 'Despite this disclaimer, he was now examining his faith, and the re-examination necessarily included some imaginative consideration of what it would be like to combat the fear of death without recourse to the Christian doctrine of immortality' (Winn 405). Elsewhere in the preface, Dryden states that he has translated Lucretius 'more happily' than he has (thus far) translated Vergil, and throughout his comments on Lucretius he seems poised on the brink of admitting his real elective affinity with the Roman atheist. But he cannot bring himself to do that because the poem he wants to but dares not translate, the poem he pilfers from and jettisons, is not fit for (saleable to and laudable by) his secular audience, much less his religious one. The other Latin pagans can be made to accord both with Christian tradition and with modern sensibilities that are in the process of disengaging themselves from that tradition. But this poem, so far from helping in the desired and necessary fusion of Christian tradition with emerging modernity that Dryden and other fellow progressive conservatives are eager for, actually spotlights the (wide and widening) chasm between old and new Europe. What the poem keeps saying (and Dryden keeps loving and hating to hear) is that the old world's values and moralities and the new world's values and moralities would not, finally, cohere (or, as he himself would force himself to put it, superbly, in the closing verses of his final composition, 'The Secular Masque': "Tis well an Old Age is out,/ And time to begin a New'). Though Dryden succeeded in misrepresenting the poem by hiding the vitality of its good tidings (the rich and moral life that the pursuit of true pleasure achieves once atomic truth has begun directing it), the form, the style, of his misrepresentations show that he understood the crossroads that he and his society had come to. If Englishmen (and Europeans) wanted men to refrain from criminality, they would have to find a new argument against it because Hell was about to disappear, and if they wanted to aspire to happiness, they would have to find a new blueprint for a new sort of Heaven (Austin 598-601).

In Creech's translation of the entire poem, what is grim about existence is reduced in exact proportion as the poet's meliorism is adequately expressed. Where Dryden's fragments magnify despair and pain (and erase joy and celebration), Creech translates what is actually there. But Creech's version, though well received in its time and capable of holding its own throughout the eighteenth century, could not finally match Dryden's for grandeur and for vigour (Fleischmann 1964, 143). And, in any case, Creech's preface and the testimonials that accompany it reassure their readers that they are in no danger of having to take what the ancient atheist has to say seriously. Creech makes Lucretius safe for Christian Readers, especially for those who are no longer entirely secure in their beliefs, by lumping the atheist poet in with other enemies of the state. And he is more interested in the poet's life than Dryden was: 'As most of the other Poets, He had his share of sensual Pleasures; nor can the poor excuse of Catullus make me think better of him when I view him in his fourth Book. And the account of his Death strengthens this opinion, for ... he dyed by his own Hands in the Fourty Fourth year of his Age, being dementated by a Philtrum given by his Mistress, tho others place his Death in the Twenty Sixth year, and believe his madness proceeded from the Cares and Melancholy that opprest him after the banishment of his beloved Memmius.' Here, as everywhere, the death is overdetermined (wicked mistress and crazy to boot), but Creech adds a new ingredient to the brew: separated from his 'beloved' Memmius when still a young man, Lucretius falls into a suicidal melancholy. Melancholy becomes a Lucretian epithet in the centuries that follow Creech's translation. It takes on, in Lucretian reception, a life of its own. And it helps Creech have the best of two worlds.

In his elaborate and pious preface he can effectively distance himself from the insane non-believer he has translated without weakening his apology for wanting to be the first to provide a complete English version of this great if dangerous poet. (He did not know that a woman,

86

3. A Genealogy of Melancholy

Lucy Hutchinson, had beaten him to the punch a few decades earlier with a translation that has only recently been published.) Despite what the Latin poet tells him, Creech understands that there are good reasons (he gives four) why God harms the innocent and seems to spare the guilty, and he knows, too, that Epicurus cannot guide us to sanity: 'And now who can imagine such absurd Principles proper to lead any rational Enquirer to Serenity? Will it be a comfort to a good man to tell him [that] … A Whirl-wind rules, when 'tis his greatest interest that there should be a merciful Disposer who takes notice of and will reward his Piety?'

If there is a tension in Dryden's preface between what he thinks about Lucretius and what his language says he feels about him, in Creech one finds a similar tension between what his preface claims to disbelieve and what the discipline and engagement of his verse indicate he may believe. Some of Creech's readers sensed that tension and some of these pointed to Creech's own depressions and suicide as evidence of the nature of his fascination with the mad poet and his poem (Fleischmann 1964, 195). But, Nahum Tate, in his charming blurb-poem at the opening of the volume, dismisses any thought of such disharmonies in the translator or his translation:

> With thine thy Country's Fame, thou here dost show
> What British speech and British speech can do.
> Lucretius Englisht! Tis so rich a prize
> We gaze upon't and scarce believe our Eyes.
> We read, and see the Roman Genius Shine,
> Without allay in each bright page of thine;
> Then pause, and doubting still, again repair,
> Again we find the learn'd Lucretius there.

There had been French translations of the poem, and John Evelyn had translated the first book, but (Hutchinson's version was unknown) Creech had done the astonishing (and patriotic) thing and provided his countrymen with a complete and English Lucretius. Furthermore, in addition to the miracle of translating this difficult (and monstrous) poem into elegant, current English, he had done something hardly less remarkable:

Thy pains oblige us on a double score,
True to thy author, to religion more,
While Learnedly his Errors thou dost note
And for his Poyson bringst an Antidote,
From Epicurus' walks thus weeding Vice,
No more the Garden but a Paradise.

The poem has been accurately and fully translated. Anyone who read English could now read Lucretius and they could also read him safely. His 'Errors' Creech had diligently spotted and copiously documented. The venom of heresy vanished when orthodox piety confronted it. Epicurus had figured his spacetime of salvation as a garden into which the bodyspirit withdraws from the world's illusions. That was an artificial paradise, the best that the pagans could manage with what they had. Tate neatly spins that image into one suitable for the sign-system of emerging English bourgeois Christianity. Creech's transfiguring translation of the old (great) pagan poem is not a garden, not that (pagan) garden at any rate. It's more of a garden weeded of its vicious growths (that would be, most of the poem), until it has been transformed into a modern Christian (English) garden (think Marvell), a natural *and* cultivated spacetime where sophisticated and humanist Christians can relax (and forget recent civil wars, and religious dissessions, and what the astronomers seem to be saying about this planet and its place in the cosmos). Nothing dreadful, nothing melancholy here: exquisite couplets, pious thoughts, civilised sentiments. That's what became of Lucretius, what he stood for, just as the pre-modern world began recognising itself. But the melancholy that Jerome had first branded on the poet's poem would continue seeping through its new and expurgated skin; as before, its readers kept projecting their own anxieties on it.

Meanwhile, across the Channel

Throughout the eighteenth century, in the nations of Europe, the men (and women) of the Enlightenment would carry about with them pocket editions of Lucretius, a Lucretius defined in large measure by the spirit that enforms the Gassendi-Dryden selections, a sanitised and invisibly abridged Lucretius (all the text was there but you knew which pages to memorise and which to close your eyes to), a Lucretius inside whose poem various tribes of modern humanism might flirt with modern Christian sensibilities. But in France, which had produced three translations of Lucretius before Creech's (Spink 103-9, 148-51), more people read more of the poem as the Enlightenment picked up steam. Though natural scientists, as they progressed in their studies, might begin to find Lucretius an embarrassing ancestor (forgetful of the role he had recently played in the shaping of their disciplines), though the more fervent hedonists might come to dismiss him as something of a prude (Fleischmann 1963, 634), his hatred of superstition and his determination to find or to invent meaning in a godless universe permeate the spirit if not the letter of the *philosophes*' efforts to rethink our place in reality.

A clear index of that wide and abiding influence is available in Cardinal Melchior de Polignac's *Anti-Lucretius: Or, On God and Nature* (1671-1742); the poem was published after his death in 1747 and a translation of it in English, by George Canning, appeared in 1767 (Hadzsits 321; the poem was published posthumously in Paris in 1747, Ament 29). The villains of the Cardinal's poem are various miscreants who purvey various styles of materialism (Hobbes, Gassendi, Newton, Locke); but, as the title of the poem signals, the corrupt minds behind them, seeding their heresies and nourishing them, are the Greek atomist and his Roman interpreter, whose poem and whose style the Cardinal knows well enough to imitate (with marked success) in Latin hexameters. Here is his opening salvo against Epicurus (Canning, 7):

> The Man, who first dard hardily to feign,
> Gods scarce existing, lazy, dull and vain,
> Who framd eternal Atoms at his will,
> By casual concourse empty space to fill,
> Who doomd to death man's noblest part, the soul,
> And gave blind chance the conduct of the whole,
> With shameless confidence, himself proclaims
> (Herald of pleasure) all his guilty aims.

Polignac sidesteps the easy mistake of confusing Lucretius and the master who corrupted *him* with atheists. Worse than atheism, their blasphemy allows for the semi-existence of deities who are 'lazy, dull and vain' (so p. 167, 'A lazy, dull, inert, inglorious breed,/ Your idle gods from casual atoms sprung'). They mock true Godhead, which has in any case been usurped by the audacious founder of the sect who reinvents ('at his will') the universe, imagining it to consist of eternal atoms and the void they move in (and fill up). This perverter of truth denies the immortality of the soul and insists that it is chance, not Providence, that guides the universe. He also professes the gospel of (sensual) pleasure, and he glories in his crimes. That neatly condenses everything in the pagan poem that offends traditional Christians, and everything that Helvétius and La Mettrie and Holbach and Diderot and Voltaire found attractive in it (well, as we'll soon see, Voltaire does have one sly objection, one that Diderot found amusing).

Polignac is keenly alert to the dangers to Christian life and thought that admiration of Lucretius entails. For him those dangers are rooted in a profound immorality that derives its powerful attractions from pure sensuality. Seduced by the promise of desires unendingly satisfied and replenished, the soul forgets whatever limits it has learned, and forgets, too, both its true origin and the goal it was created to strive for. Hidden by the mask of this glittering species of hedonism is the face of moral and rational decadence. In this powerful misreading of Lucretian pleasure, wicked carnality and arrogant misreason enter into a fateful alliance whose mutual corruptions endanger European culture and Christendom itself:

> Led by Gassendi, some would fain defend
> Their favorite Sage's doctrine, and pretend
> That no vain Pleasure Epicurus sought
> But prizd alone the joy which Virtue brought.
> Such men, deceivd by specious sounds, applaud
> Th'Imposter's semblance, nor detect his fraud.
> Virtue's his constant theme, but all the time,
> Virtue's a cloke, to cover every crime. (p. 33)

Those whom Epicurus and Gassendi have duped blather on about serenity as the fruit of virtue's greatest pleasure and best reward, but the Cardinal knows how slippery that primrose path is – for any age group, but particularly for the young:

90

Some youth who draughts from your black fountain drains
And feels the potent poison in his veins,
Spurning religion, loosed from every fear ...
Say what can curb him should he hope to shroud
His flagrant crimes in secrecy's dark cloud?
Can robbery, rape, or murder shake his soul,
Hid from men's eyes, his soul's confessd controul?
Ardent to follow, panting to obey,
Wher'er his Goddess, PLEASURE, points the way .... (p. 11)

Polignac knows that it is young people who feel pleasure most fiercely and are therefore most vulnerable to the temptations of wicked hedonism. As it turns out, the Cardinal's own Memmius (named Quintius in his poem) is just such a youth: 'But *Quintius*, you, whom Pleasure, linkd with youth,/ Has snatchd incautious from the path of truth ...'. In his inexperience, callow Quintius, venturing near the Lucretian arcadia, is in danger of hearing and enjoying the poet's bad song and its alluring lies:

In the recess of some refrigerant cave,
With rapture listening, hear SILENUS rave;
As every vein while Nectar's juice inflames,
With stammering tongue the drunken God declaims
Of seeds dispersed through vacuous realms he sings,
And how from Hazard's Sport all Being springs. (p. 339)

As drunk with poetry as the drunken poet-god who sings of chaos as if it were paradise, the innocent youth might tarry there ('Claspd in Illusion's Soft encircling arms,/ Blind is the libertine to Virtue's charms', p. 337), ready to assent to the poet's worst blasphemy: 'Grant me all these' (the atoms) 'obedient to my nod,/ And straight I'll build a world without a God' (p. 337).

Mere carnalities might be almost innocent if they did not pave the way to intellectual sins. In Polignac's lifetime, the youth of Europe has been encouraged (mostly by Gassendi) to read and accept the *DRN* not only as a beautiful poem with noble sentiments and exquisite sights and sounds but also as a document that contains (some) wisdom and (some) truth. The effect of this insidious process has been disastrous, because, while learning scepticism about revealed truth from this text, the young libertines also imbibe its fatal dogmas.

Whether started and spread by design or by accident, the proof of the poem's bad success is the constellation of brilliant minds that have been infected by the poet whose name gives the Cardinal's poem its title, the small army of perverted talents that have elaborated those antique lies to corrupt others. Polignac imagines Lucretius, like a Roman General, celebrating his wicked triumph:

> While Nations charmd attend his magick song
> And vanquished Gods in chains are dragged along,
> Religion follows, weeping, captive, bound,
> A choir of pious mourners sorrowing sound,
> Till to the altar led the victim stands,
> There doomed to fall by sacrilegious hands.
> Lo! the mad Youth in riot loud advance
> With scornful jest obscene and wanton dance ... (238)

Polignac's replacing of the pagan poet's Iphigenia with Religion as victim at the altar is a neat and characteristic touch, and we note that once again it is Youth that gets the emphasis and represents the real danger to Religion (older and wiser men are supposedly less susceptible to the wiles of sensual intellectual corruption). Nevertheless, despite all the fanfare, the victory of Untruth is short-lived. In fact, it is, was, a mirage.

> But thou, my Quintius, Reason for thy guide,
> Hast seen the wretched downfall of his Pride,
> Hast seen, with mingled scorn, surprize and shame,
> Th'illusion vanish, like an idle dream.
> And all the pompous triumphs of his Muse
> In empty smoke their spurious splendors lose.
> Whence, thinkst thou, principles so far from true,
> Whose inconsistence glares upon the view,
> Forming a system so absurd could find
> So general credit with abus'd Mankind?
> Twas fell DESIRE, that aided his pretence,
> Pander of Falsehood, Parasite of Sense.

Desire and the falsehoods it generates, the parasitical empiricism that aids carnality to construct its counterfeits of rational truth – all these, bit by bit, the Cardinal's poem dissects, slowly, patiently, passionately. 'Thus arm'd by Reason, Piety o'erthrows/ The atomick System, with redoubled blows' (319), until the Cardinal can announce to the arrogant poet: 'I see 'tis over: vanquish'd in the field,/ By Reason's prowess, thou'rt compell'd to yield' (420).

Having claimed that victory, he is free to confiscate the pagan poem's vision and transform it for a modern Christian world. He too can gaze on the immensity of the universe and feel its grandeur:

> But when at once, with all its rolling spheres
> To my Mind's eye the Universe appears,
> Absorb'd in thought, the power I seek in vain,
> Searching through every region of my brain,
> The power, whose wisdom, providence and care,
> Form'd all those images and fix'd them there:
> My life's duration would not ev'n suffice
> To view distinctly, with corporeal eyes,
> The various crowd of objects, which I find
> By Power unseen impressed upon my Mind. (425)

The Cardinal looks up at the same sky that had seized Lucretius with a holy pleasure and a shivering awe. What escaped the Lucretian gaze, what other recent gazers, misled by Lucretius, had also missed (relying only on 'corporeal eyes' and materialist brains), the Cardinal apprehends with the eyes of faith. Or rather, he cannot comprehend it with corporeal eyes. A lifetime's looking at these wonders with fleshly eyes would not suffice to reveal the invisible power that wrought that miracle, which, both unseen and unknown, is nevertheless 'impressed upon' his 'Mind'. This is a forceful conclusion to a forceful poem, one whose remarkable virtues derive both from its reluctant appreciation of its model/target and from its frightened awareness of how pervasive the poet and poem it challenges had become in the modern world, how well that poem answered the evolving modern temper, how deep and how intricate its influence had been and might continue to be.

But the Cardinal was preaching to the converted. Humanists went right on reading Lucretius, though not for reasons that would have worried Polignac. They continued reading him, seldom from cover to cover, for their favourite purple passages, for the poetry's sights and sounds, for the moral uplift they discovered in him and, covertly, for the vigour and fun of his denunciations of superstition. His 'science', however, was becoming increasingly archaic and people began to forget how crucial he had been to the construction of the scientific temper they were now enjoying. By the time *Anti-Lucretius* was published, and certainly by the time Canning published his translation of it, Lucretius' 'influence' had become almost transparent, almost invisible. The poem was no longer a clarion call, it was part of the furniture.

But for Denis Diderot (1713-1784) it was much more than that, it was, for his masterpiece, catalytic. In 1769, twenty-two years after the appearance of Polignac's poem, Diderot wrote the three dialogues that bear the central one's title, *D'Alembert's Dream*. The work was so scandalous that it was not published until 1831, long after the author's death. He had already used a quotation from Lucretius (*quae sunt in luce tuemur e tenebris*, we look from darkness at what the light shines on) as the motto for an earlier composition (*The Interpretation of Nature,* 1753), and the year before he wrote the *Dream* he had helped edit and provide the commentary for a new translation of *DRN* (that of La Grange: Wilson 18, 559; Fusil 162). Thus, his brain freshly teeming with Lucretius, he undertook his funny and (still) astonishing meditation on the cosmos, how it works and what it may, or may not, add up to.

In the first dialogue, a card-carrying materialist (Diderot) energetically and wittily debates the nature of things with a timorous, half-hearted materialist (D'Alembert). In the second dialogue, D'Alembert's mistress discusses with his doctor (another full-fledged materialist) the surreal contents of her companion's delirious dream of the previous night, fragments of which she managed to jot down as he muttered and raved them; still dreaming or, later, roused from his sleep, D'Alembert interrupts their discussion from time to time with frantic observations of his own. In the third dialogue, having lunched, the mistress and the doctor return to the subjects that had engrossed them in the morning, now paying close attention to various sexual topics – onanism, same-sexuality, cross-breeding. It's worth noting that, at the close of this dialogue, the doctor tells an anecdote in which

Cardinal Polignac has an unexpected cameo: he offers to baptise an orangutang 'in a glass cage that looks like St John preaching in the desert', if it speaks: *Parle et je vous baptise.*

The scientific and philosophical speculations to which these dialogues give comic form concern themselves with the problems of how life originated, how it developed through the aeons from simple to complex forms, and how the human brain-mind arose from matter and mere sentience. Different though most of his arguments are from those of Lucretius, Diderot, throughout the dialogues, remains true to one of his chief inspirations for them, the one proffered him by the poem whose most recent translation he had assisted in preparing for publication. Arthur Wilson offers this elegant description of that inspiration's core:

> Anyone setting himself the task of explaining the origin of the cosmos has a choice of three philosophical stances from which to proceed. He can say that in the beginning was the idea; as the Christians say, in the beginning was the Word. Theories of Creation fall within this idealist position. Or he can predicate the dualist position, holding that both spirit and matter are primal. This was the position taken by Descartes. Finally, there is the conception, the materialist one, that only matter is primal, and that somehow or other the cosmos took shape, including Adam and Eve, without the intervention of a Creator. Just how this could happen is what *Le rêve de d'Alembert* is about. Lucretius had gone over this ground and Diderot followed him in his uncompromising materialism. (561-2)

Implicit in this vision of a universe uncreated and aimless is an insistence that all of its phenomena can and must be represented in purely physical terms and that its transcendence (for want of another word) consists only in its (ungraspable) totality, in the incalculable sum of its parts. It is the vision that Polignac had glimpsed with horror and tried to efface. Something of the power and beauty of its counter-metaphysics, of its carnal spirituality, informs these sentences from Isak Dinesen's 'The Monkey':

> The real difference between God and human beings – that God cannot stand continuance and human beings cling to existing

things. Their art is nothing but the attempt to catch by any means the particular moment – and make it everlasting. It is wrong to imagine paradise as a never-changing state of bliss. It will probably turn out to be, in the true spirit of God, an incessant whirlwind.

Substitute Nature for God in this passage and you have the essence of Diderot's (long unpublished) rejection of Christianity and of the metaphysical traditions that sustain it; you have also something of the spirit that shapes his celebration of the truth of the whirlwind, of the 'divine' pleasure and shivering, and of the dynamic reality that gives the lie to 'the fallacy of the ephemeral', the belief of creatures of the day in the permanence of what they leave behind them when they 'go'.

As Christians see it, God's human creatures lose their ephemerality and the world's when divine grace has translated them, beyond their deaths, into celestial immutability. Diderot is at his most Lucretian when he rejects this style of cosmic comfort and praises instead the ephemerality of everything. From this perspective, where nothing endures except atoms and the void, where only the processes of coming to be and passing away are unending, our longing for permanence, though understandable, is a futile misuse of our brains and our energies.

The cool scepticism that D'Alembert evinced in the first dialogue gives way in the second to a frenzy of babblings and mutterings which screen (even as they clearly reveal) Diderot's materialist speculations. Like Buster Keaton released from silence, like one of Beckett's baffled creatures grown suddenly ecstatic, the voice behind the speakers of these dialogues lets their language explode with astonished admiration for a universe that Lucretius could easily recognise for his own. Joyfully ephemeral, the speeches in the dialogue give voice to their writer's 'new', materialist perspective on self-in-world:

I am what I am because that's how it had to be. Alter the cosmos and you alter me as well. Because everything is changing, always, everywhere ... All the species circulate, they mingle, mesh and mix, the one with the other, and that's why each of nature's kinds is – what? – everythings's in motion, always on the go ... You silly philosophers, always jabbering about essences! ... Life?

3. A Genealogy of Melancholy

What is Life but a series of actions and reactions? ... Being born, living, dying – what's that but shifting shapes? Every configuration of matter has the well-being and the grief that suits it. Start with the elephant and end with the flea – or start with the flea and go all the way down to the living, sentient molecule, germ of everything that is – there's nothing in all nature that is incapable of suffering or delight.

Lucretius knows nothing of sentient molecules; Diderot corrects the Roman's 'mechanistic atom' with a 'special kind of atom capable of becoming something akin to what would now be called a cell', 'a building block that could be vitalistic, compatible with the properties of life' (Wilson 562). Otherwise this world is essentially the one he bequeathed to Diderot, the world that Diderot has modernised, has corrected in the light of 'contemporary advances'.

Ian Smith, to whom we are principally indebted for uncovering what is Lucretian in Diderot, remarks of this passage, perhaps for rhetorical effect: 'It is curious that this vision, where not only the individual is seen as impermanent, but the species, the earth, and heaven itself, should have the power of provoking exaltation and enthusiasm' (Smith 133). Yes, 'curious' if your worldview is creationist and teleological, if it is defined by divine origins and divine last things. But if you live in a world where that pattern of seeing, thinking and valuing seems alien, then perhaps Lucretius and his best heir can speak to you. But the last word on this subject belongs to Smith, who knows how both writers 'are charged with the same enthusiasm, the same wonderment at the boundless and unending play of matter, at its infinite variety and possibilities', 134. He goes on, handsomely:

Many of Lucretius' arguments didn't satisfy Diderot, just as today Diderot's theories no longer satisfy us. And yet, just as Diderot felt the impact of Lucretius' intense conviction and the poetic force of his language, so today Diderot can evoke the enthusiasm of the modern reader even though he may not share his naive trust in the experiments of Needham [a proponent of spontaneous generation who examined organisms under a microscope]. Materialism has inspired few poets, yet perhaps, no less

than any other system, it merits the prestige of poetic expression;
in this regard it has been amply served by Lucretius and Diderot.

(For a more traditional view of Diderot's Lucretius, see Mason 45, 52,
219, 257-8, 307.)

Two years after Diderot wrote his *Dream*, Voltaire published his
'Letters of Memmius to Cicero' (1771). This droll composition cannot
be an answer to Diderot (since Diderot did not publish the dream
dialogues in his lifetime, nor is it likely that Voltaire even knew of
them), but it is unquestionably a riposte to the *philosophes* around
Diderot who were disappointed by what they took to be Voltaire's
wobbly stand on what can be called the project of materialism. When
the chips were down, Voltaire opted for a witty Deism (Aldridge 368-9).

His preface reminds the reader that Lucretius' 'lovely poem' was
written 'to shape the mind and heart of Gaius Memmius Gemellus, a
young man of great expectations from one of the best families of Rome'.
It turned out, however, that Memmius, as his letters to Cicero clearly
indicate, became a better philosopher than his teacher. The long-lost
manuscript of the letters was discovered, claims the preface, in the
Vatican Library by a Russian admiral (Sheremetof) who translated
them into Russian 'in order to shape the minds and hearts of his
nephews'. The writer of the preface, having been unable to consult the
Vatican manuscript, has made his French translation from the Russian version. He is sure, nevertheless, that both his version and its
source faithfully reflect their original because the spirit of antique
Rome is everywhere manifest in them (no forgeries here). The writer
of the preface admits that 'the philosophy of Memmius is somewhat
audacious (*hardie*), but in this he hardly differs from Cicero himself
and other great men of antiquity (who had the common misfortune of
not having read the *Summa* of Aquinas)'. For all that, he continues,
one never fails to discover in those antique writings 'shafts of sunlight
that furnish us with great pleasure'.

Memmius' first letter to Cicero is occasioned by news of the death of
his 'friend', Lucretius. The event grieves him but does not suprise him:
'he is freed from the sorrows of a life which he could no longer endure;
his miseries were incurable'. His (melancholy) friend's all too understandable decision to kill himself has prompted Memmius to reread
his *DRN*, 'through which he will live eternally' (thus disproving his

98

notions of mortality, but Memmius doesn't spoil his irony by mentioning that). 'Once upon a time he wrote that poem for me,' continues Memmius, 'but the disciple was estranged from his master. Neither you nor I, Cicero, belong to his cult.' Naughty Voltaire! His contemporaries were doubtless astonished to learn from this recently discovered text that Memmius had joined Cicero in the New Academy, a sort of Platonising Scepticism fortified, in Cicero's case, with a strong dash of Stoicism. Thus Lucretius is here slandered by his former student, and his teachings are betrayed. Nevertheless, having looked again (for old times' sake) at the silly book, Memmius decides to write a sustained critique of it, which he promises to share with his new friend, Cicero.

We learn from the second letter that Cicero has written back to affirm how much he likes Lucretius' poem, as well as his descriptions of nature and his moral sentiments and, above all, 'what he says against superstition'. With these typical eighteenth-century judgments Memmius agrees wholeheartedly. In fact, 'if his pronouncements on natural science were not as ridiculous as every one else's, it would be godlike'. Where he principally differs with his former master, we learn in the third letter, is on questions of theology. He says it straight out: he does not believe in gods (like Epicurus and Lucretius) but he does believe in God (so much for scepticism). Lots of philosophers are going to hiss at him for admitting this (perhaps Diderot and his circle?), they will call him a weak sister (*esprit faible*: Diderot had in fact just called him that). But he forgives them for their godless materialism and begs them, with superb charity, to pardon him for his weakness.

The core of his piety is a commensensical and ubiquitous instinct, humankind's feeling that 'this world is designed by a supreme intelligence'. Memmius denounces the mad fantasy that the world could come into being through chance and centres his refutation of it on an appeal to Plato's Eternal Geometer. Behind all the variety and plenitude of the universe (Memmius forgets to mention that Lucretius hymns that fertile dynamism frequently and unforgettably) there must be 'a sublime artist ... an intelligence enormously superior to our own because it has made what we are barely capable of understanding. And this intelligence, this power – that is what I call God.' (Note that Memmius' estimates of the limits of our mind-brain are more generous than those of, say, McGinn: 134-7, 173-4, 214.)

The remaining letters are mostly devoted to arguments against enemies of creationism and to speculations on the nature of the human soul and its relationship with its Maker. But, no less certain than his own maker that there must be a Poet behind the Poem (the Sublime Artist), Memmius recoups the full force of his style of doubting when he comes to examine hypotheses about the nature of the soul (if they were with us today, both he and Lucretius might agree to call it consciousness) and about its immortality and its chances of knowing divine things. Every definition of the soul is ruthlessly interrogated and summarily dismissed ('so many cults, so many imaginations, so many chimeras', Letter 13). All Memmius knows of this matter is that the Maker knew what He was doing: He gave us everything we need to learn all we need to know about ourselves and Him and Reality. Memmius is dubious about the prospects of our immortality and is downright contemptuous about the likelihood of metempsychosis. He believes, however, that morality is innate in our kind, and he thanks Cicero for having written so eloquently of 'precepts of virtue so deeply engraved in the human heart by nature's own hand' that all the priests in the world, barbarian and Roman alike, have not been able to erase them. He is worried about the state of the Roman Republic, but he feels it probably deserves to perish. Nevertheless, he hopes that, after things degenerate still further and bad tyrants get even worse, things will eventually improve and 'good masters' will arise. This lucky new breed of men, if they read Cicero's works, will become virtuous, that is, obedient to their good leaders. These cheerful sentiments console him (Memmius and Voltaire) for all the troubles he's seen and all the troubles he foresees.

That would be a good place to end this satire on the hard core materialism of Diderot and Company, those closet-Epicureans who find him and his style of creationism so quaint. But he (Memmius, Voltaire) has to write one last letter. While visiting Alexandria, Memmius, Platonic convert and Lucretian apostate, had the occasion (or misfortune) to see some Miracle Workers close up and in action. These crazy ascetics and their faith healings are all the rage in the mysterious East, and their appalling popularity has caused Memmius to start worrying. Suppose these madmen should someday chance to fuse their loathing of life with Plato's transcendental yearnings: that vital (and maybe fatal) hybridity could spell real trouble for the religion of the

100

empire, and if those zealots, emboldened by Platonic gibberish, should band together and challenge the status quo and win out – well, *that* revolution could lead in turn to an endless proliferation of holy wars, a chain reaction of religious mayhem that might well continue for centuries. Human beings (despite their moral hearts) are so superstitious, so insane, and so wicked (once religion has sunk its fangs into them) that this prognosis seems a likely one. What he really fears is a time when one sect persecutes other sects, when they start persecuting their own. Doubtful that any prayer avails against these terrors, he nevertheless begs the great (Platonic) Demiurge to avert this. Where Lucretius wants superstition stamped out, the Ciceronian humanist would settle for religious tolerance. He has the sinking feeling that once the bad habit of religious persecution begins it will turn earth into a worse hell than any poet ever painted.

Using Memmius as his dummy (rather as Diderot had used D'Alembert as his) Voltaire thus ventriloquises his objections to the radical materialism of the Encyclopedists who have twitted him with godly hankerings. He likes Lucretius' unpersuadable anger against the disease of superstition but is irritated by his implicit denunciations of Voltaire's own style of deistic, civilised humanism. And he is no longer in the mood to listen to mind-boggling arguments that compel the human mind to perform contortions it was never *intended* to perform: that the Book of Nature needs no Author, that it writes Itself with no notion of what it is doing, that thinking creatures need no Creator to design their minds for them. So he sends Lucretius a small ironic valentine, one that he hopes will really piss off Holbach and Diderot (Aldridge 362).

*

Polignac, Diderot and Voltaire represent, among them, the major versions of the figure of Lucretius in their own century, and they foreshadow what will become of that figure in the centuries that follows theirs: Lucretius as the scapegoat of creationism; Lucretius as the standard-bearer of pure materialism; and, once he'd been shaved, perfumed and powdered, Lucretius as the harbinger of a genteel and culturally viable, culturally nurturing deism. For our immediate purposes, it is sufficient to note that the ever popular depressive (and manic) suicide disappears entirely from view in Diderot's farcical and passionate presentation of pure materialism where he is evoked, anonymously and safely, and allowed to revel shamelessly in the pleasures of his uncut materialism. In Polignac also, who focuses on the sensual atheist whom Epicurus seduced and on the insane hybris that prompts his irreligiosity, there is no room for the mere melancholiac. But in Voltaire, we watch the ill-bred atheist's most prominent disciple react to the news of his death in much the same way as a distinguished novelist once reacted to the death of a rival ('he has made a wise career decision'), and on this funny and vicious page, the sign-system that produced the modern version of the melancholy madman discloses itself most clearly: secular humanism could not allow one of its earliest and most eloquent spokesmen to join in its progress towards modernity without castigating his unfortunate excesses. That (excessive, authentic) Lucretius even Diderot relegated to posthumous publication because in the world of the good bourgeois the poet of the *DRN* has to be expurgated in order to flourish inside the canon. It is from the interplay of these three perspectives on Lucretius – wicked materialist, noble materialist, madman on medication = genteel humanist – that our modern Lucretius emerges after his later, more dramatic reinventions in the nineteenth century.

4

The Anti-Lucretius Himself

Did I not believe that an Intelligence is at the heart of things, my
life on earth would be intolerable.   Carlyle

Back across the Channel

In the fourth edition of the *Encyclopaedia Britannica* (1810) we read
that

> Lucretius, one of the most celebrated of the Latin poets, was born
> of an ancient and noble Roman family, and studied at Athens,
> where he became one of Epicurus' sect. He acquired great repu-
> tation by his learning and eloquence; but in the flower of his age
> fell into a frenzy, occasioned by a philtre given him by his wife,
> who was distractedly fond of him. Lucretius, during the intervals
> of his madness, put Epicurus' doctrines into verse, and composed
> his six books *De Rerum Natura*, which are still extant. It is said
> that he killed himself in a fit of madness, in the 54th year before
> the Christian era, when 51 years old. The most correct edition of
> Lucretius is that of Simon de Coline. The cardinal de Polignac
> has refuted Lucretius' arguments in his excellent Latin poem
> entitled *Anti-Lucretius*. His poem *De Rerum Natura* has been
> translated into English by Mr Creech.

The details about the poet's origins, early education and early success,
joined with an estimation of his wife's passion for him ('distractedly' is
a delicious detail), conspire to fashion a sad tale of ruined genius. But
the poet's suicide, a half a century before his saviour's birth, is less
pathetic than poetically just, for although the lasting 'madness' in
whose interludes the godless poem was written was chemically induced and therefore innocent, we don't have to read deeply between

103

the lines to see that this death was earned. We know this because, after we are told how best to go about reading him, we are informed why it is that we need not bother to do so. Cardinal Polignac (he is still being read) has cast the poem and its errors – here oddly unspecified – into outer darkness. It's interesting to note that Byron, writing in 1818, offers ironic affirmation to this stern verdict on the poem when discussing the young Don Juan's inappropriate classical readings: 'Lucretius' irreligion is too strong/ For early stomachs, to prove wholesome food', *Don Juan* 1.43; elsewhere, though the poem shows few explicit Lucretian allusions, it abounds with the deconstructive struggle between materialism and enlightenment deism which is vividly displayed in the *Detached Thoughts*, October 1821.

Just over three decades later (1842), in the 7th edition of the *Britannica*, the entry for Lucretius has more than tripled in length and has changed its emphasis and its tone. We are told that there is 'no precise information respecting his parents, his education, or the circumstances of his life'. The entry's author then sketches the turbulent political context in which the poem was composed and cites 'an ingenious writer' who 'has attempted to draw a parallel between those horrible times and the peculiar doctrines which Lucretius advocated. It is said that, not daring to attribute the misery of his country to the justice and wisdom of the gods, he was anxious to dethrone a Providence which seemed to abandon the world to the passions of ambitious tyrants.' The author mentions, but seems unpersuaded by, a tradition that the poem 'was composed during the lucid intervals of a madness caused by a love potion which had been administered to him by his wife Lucilia'. He suppresses the suicide, and passes on to a finely nuanced and sympathetic estimate of the poet's talents and his achievement. He praises the poet's 'skilful manner' 'even when his subject 'does not admit of poetical embellishment' and 'the dignity with which he unfolds his philosophical views'. He shows a discriminating admiration for the poem's style. He singles out for special praise 'the introductory parts of each book' (everybody's favourite purples) but surprisingly adds to these 'the description of the plague of Athens'. He notes that the 'invocation to Venus' and 'the powerful description of love' are among 'the most celebrated passages ... but, to form a just idea of his talents we must read the fifth book, in which he narrates the formation of society'. This author has read and is reading the entire poem. Listen to his conclusion:

> His philosophy is that of the atheist; he denies the existence of a Deity and of a Providence; he disbelieves in the immortality of the soul, and laughs at the idea of death. From the depths of this heartless scepticism, *however*, he darts at times to the very heights of enthusiasm and poetry. But the character of his system experiences no change. He destroys all those gods with whom the poets loved to people the universe; he ridicules the idea of a future life, and of future rewards and punishments; he represses all hopes and stifles all fear; *yet* all ages have admired this poem of Lucretius, as one of the most wonderful productions of human genius. (The italics are mine.)

The author misunderstands or misrepresents the abiding canonicity of the *DRN*, but his *however* and his *yet* indicate something beyond a fervent aesthetic pleasure in the poem. The 'heartless scepticism' may worry him, but not as much as it worries the readers whom he's trying to coax into ignoring what they've been told in school or from the pulpit; nor does it propel him into imagining that the poem's formal beauties can be cut loose from its frightening contents. Perhaps the poem has scared him (as it was designed to do), but he has sufficiently mastered his alarm to begin rescuing the poem from its fragments and from its bad reputation. In this reading of the poem, the melancholiac has vanished along with the creationist imperative that wants him punished and the genteel humanism that wants him mollified. This version of the poem is close to Diderot's, just at the moment when Christianity and Materialism are about to clash violently.

But before we turn to that crucial moment we should first flashforward to a final *Britannica* entry, one written when the dust of the battle between the pastors and the scientists had almost settled. In the 9th Edition (1879-1888) W.Y. Sellar has procured over twelve columns for Lucretius because 'more than any of the great Roman writers' he 'has acquired a new interest in the present day'. It is not 'the force and purity of his style, nor the majesty and pathos of his poetry' that have increased interest in him. Rather, it is 'the relation of his subject to many of the questions on which speculative curiosity is now engaged'.

Although neither Lucretius nor the ancient philosophers he makes use of anticipated 'the more advanced scientific hypotheses of modern times', 'it is in his poem that we find the most complete account of the chief effort of the ancient mind to explain the beginning of things, and to understand the course of nature and man's relation to it.' For Sellar's contemporaries, these are burning issues, not least because of the 'old war between science and theology, which has been revived in the present generation'; the white-heat of Lucretius' relevance to modern times derives from his closing with these topics with the 'same ardent and uncompromising spirit' that 'living thinkers' bring to bear on them. This seems a promising line of inquiry, one that would easily account for the enormous gain in space the ancient atomist has achieved in this (modern) edition of the encyclopaedia. Yet having established this rhetorical advantage, Sellar veers suddenly away from it: 'But this concurrence with the stream of speculation in the present day is really the least of his permanent claims on the attention of the world.' Mere relevance does not interest the philologist, whose interests (and values) gravitate to what is universal and eternal. Lucretius 'both among ancient and modern writers is unique. No one else combines in the same degree the contemplative enthusiasm of a philosopher, the earnest purpose of a reformer and moral teacher, and the profound pathos and sense of beauty of a great poet.' (Note that the scientist has been elided into the philosopher, and the anti-theist-deist materialist has dissolved into the moralist and the poet.)

Fair enough, but right now Sellar is not much concerned with what Lucretius thought. What he wants us to know first is something about the genius of this poet who was capable of this uniqueness, about the teachers or 'early impressions or experience [that] gave *so sombre a colouring* to his view of life' (here and later, the italics are mine). What produced the reclusive communer with nature or the indignant satirist? 'We should like also to know how far the serene heights which he professed to have attained procured him exemption from or alleviation of the actual sorrow of life.' (A self-help book: if it really worked for him, perhaps it will work for us.) Alas, much as we want to know these things, 'there is no ancient poet, with the exception of Homer, of whose history so little is positively known'. The poet obeyed too well 'the maxim of his master, "Pass through life unnoticed" ', and he is one of those who 'do not wish to be known even while living'. He warns us that we must accept the tattered and faded fragments of this biography 'with a certain reserve'. Yet oddly enough, even after we have finished sifting vainly through the improbabilities devised by 'the enemies of Epicureanism', we are not led 'to the absolute rejection of the story' (the love-philtre, the madness, the suicide) 'as a pure invention of a hostile and uncritical age. The *evidence* afforded by the poem rather leads to the conclusion that the tradition contains some germ of fact.' We should not, then, cut off all speculation 'about the love-philtre, nor even about the recurring fits of insanity, *in the ordinary sense of the word*'. The poet's English editor, Mr Munro, was the first to observe 'that in more than one passage of his poem he writes with *extraordinary vividness of the impression produced both by dreams and by waking visions*'. We infer 'that he himself may have been *liable to such hallucinations*, which are said to be consistent with perfect sanity, though they may be the *precursors* either of *madness* or a state of *despair* and *melancholy* which often ends in *suicide*'. The poet's several statements about the urgency of his poetic project and his constant devotion to it 'produce the impression of an *unrelieved strain of mind and feeling*, which could lead in turn to some extreme reaction of spirit or some failure of intellectual power, from the consciousness of which he may, in accordance with examples which he himself quotes, *have taken refuge in suicide*'. All this would be proof enough that the improbable lies of the Christians might turn out to be God's Truth after all. But there is more. The poem is incomplete (very incomplete, the more one regards it). Who but a suicidal madman could have failed to finish that unique poem?

These thoughts on madness and suicide break off suddenly because the poem's imperfections and incompletion remind Sellar of how Cicero, godfather of Latin Philology, came to the madman's botched manuscript with his ministrations. After this, Sellar returns to what we know (or rather, don't) about the poet's life – his place of origin, his class, his milieu, his love of the countryside, his hatred of violence, his love of literature, his 'true humanity', his 'tender sympathy for human sorrow' (Vergil alone can vie with him 'in reverence for the sanctities of human feeling').

Having said all he can say about Lucretius (we are now at the bottom of the sixth of ten and a half columns of print), Sellar turns to the poem itself. Pre-eminent among its models is Empedocles. From

107

the fragments of the Greek's philosophical poem we can see that in the *DRN* 'many of its ideas and expressions have been reproduced' and that 'the same tone of impassioned solemnity and *melancholy* seem to have pervaded both works'. Yet whatever his debts to Empedocles and other Greeks (or for that matter, to Epicurus) his unique achievement was to have fused scientific speculation with moral teaching and poetic power; it was this 'interdependence' that guaranteed him his place at the summit of poetry. The rest of Sellar's description of the poem's contents and its poetic virtues is often judicious in its emphasis and impressive in its powers of sympathy with (much of) the poem. But Sellar explains away, when he does not simply ignore, the poem's sustained exultation of 'the doctrine of pleasure', and he challenges the accusation of atheism by insisting that in the poem's 'imaginative recognition of an ordering, all-pervading, all regulating power' (Nature), we find something that approaches the 'higher conceptions of modern theism' (he may mean, but not wish to say, deism?), and goes so far as to claim: 'The supposed "atheism" of Lucretius proceeds from a more deeply reverential spirit than that of the majority of professed believers in all times.' What gives the poem's style its 'majestic and elevated tone' is its 'recognition of the truth that the beauty of the world, the unceasing life and movement in nature, the destructive as well as the beneficent forces of the elements, the whole wonder and pathos of human existence, are themselves manifestations of secret invisible agencies and of eternal and immutable laws'.

That is well said, except that one gets the sense here that something like Voltaire's deity has been smuggled back into the premises through a side entrance even as Pleasure has been shown out through the front door. Genteel humanism in its latest guise has spruced up the raw materialist well enough to pass him off as (some kind of) a believer, for behind those 'invisible agencies' and 'eternal laws' there is enough of a mysterious origin to satisfy all but the most rabid creationist; and it has banished the loud hedonist, for empire, commerce and duty have no room for the gospel of pleasure and tolerate only mild and healthy diversions.

And the suicidal madman – where is he? By this time, Sellar hopes he has been forgotten. Unlike pleasure, his existence cannot be denied (there's all that evidence scattered about, right there in the text itself). Moreover, the godless materialist, the manic suicide, cannot be modernised, reformulated. The melancholy, the hallucinations, and athe-istic despair are like a stench or a scream: they are present in the poem, they are almost tangible, they can't be changed. They can only be glimpsed and forgotten.

Still, they linger on under the surface of Sellar's entry and cause its halves not to cohere. But it is more than this almost invisible tension between Sellar's exemplary (modern, deistic) humanist and his an-tique madman doppelgänger that permits the latter to overwhelm the former. The madman sticks in the mind here, while the good pagan fades from it, because he has powerful help not only from his long history (from Jerome onwards) but also from his recent, unforgettable performance in one of Tennyson's most brilliant poems.

It's alive, it's alive

In 1859, Matthew Arnold had been appalled to discover that Lucretius was his contemporary (Turner 334), finding that the 'depression and *ennui*' that he saw 'stamped on how many of the representative works of modern time!' were 'stamped as well on the poems of Lucretius'. This decadent's 'melancholy' shows 'a rigid and moody gloom', that is worse in its way than Vergil's mopings. Given that stern rejection, we are surprised by a passage in a letter to his mother written six years later:

> I am rather troubled to find that Tennyson is at work on a subject, the story of the Latin poet Lucretius, which I have been occupied on for some twenty years ... Every one, except the few friends who have known I had it in hand, will think I borrowed the subject from him. So far from this, I suspect the subject was put into his head by Palgrave, who knew I was busy with it. I shall probably go on, however, but it is annoying.

His rival, who had in fact been perusing the new edition of *DRN* by H.A.J. Munro, had 'stolen a march on him' (Thorn 366-7), and, unluck-ily for Arnold, this dramatic monologue, though it offers plenty of melancholy and gloom, is far from being rigid. It is lava from the volcano in full flow. There is nothing here of Browning's leisurely, hairpin zigzags and patient nuances. Tennyson begins *in medias res* and is soon ready for the steep plunge to his frightening catastrophe

109

(Rudd 104). 'Lucilia, wedded to Lucretius, found/ Her master cold ...'.
In twenty-five verses her marital discontent, her daring solution to it
and its luckless aftermath are rapidly sketched. He once desired her;
he says he loves her still, but to his wife this seems not to be the case:
'often when the woman heard his foot/ return from pacings in the field',
he was too preoccupied (apparently with the form and contents of the
DRN) to respond to her kisses. One time too many, with no kiss for her,
he ends his constitutional by hurrying off to the library ('To turn and
ponder those three hundred scrolls/ Left by the Teacher whom he held
divine'). Finally fed up, suspecting that he's cheating on her, she
rushes off to a witch to buy a philtre:

> And this, at times, she mingled with his drink,
> And this destroy'd him; for the wicked broth
> Confused the chemic labour of the blood,
> And tickling the brute brain within the man's
> Made havock among those tender cells, and check'd
> His power to shape: he loath'd himself; and once
> After a tempest woke upon a morn
> That mock'd him with returning calm, and cried:
> 'Storm of the night! ...'

That 'once' almost gets lost in the rapid syntax of the opening narrative
that sets up his speech (so too, the 'at times' above it, and the 'often'
before that). By the time we find ourselves inside his monologue with
him he has had an accumulation of bouts of madness followed by
sanity restored (those famous lucid intervals in which the poem is
written). Crucial here are the brute brain contrasted with the human
brain (shades of Jekyll and Hyde), the self-loathing and the elegant
pathos of the victim's 'tender cells' (the 'modern' term gestures ironically to the ancient poet's archaic scientific vocabulary). Tennyson has
chosen the moment when the doomed poet's sane mind is just beginning to be able to try (in vain) to confront its ruination:

> Storm, and what dreams, ye holy Gods, what dreams!
> For thrice I waken'd after dreams ...

The cry to the Gods is peculiar: either he has temporarily forgotten

110

that gods don't hear the cries of mortals or he is so shaken by current difficulties that he reverts to the primitive superstitions of his contemporaries which, in his poem, he is busy trying to annihilate.

The dreams, in any case, were 'terrible'. In the first of these, it seemed to him that

> A void was made in Nature; all her bonds
> Crack'd; and I saw the flaring atom-streams
> And torrents of her myriad universe,
> Ruining along the illimitable inane,
> Fly on and crash together again, and make
> Another and another frame of things
> For ever: that was mine, my dream, I knew it
> Of and belonging to me ...

Nature is *made* of void (and atoms), a void cannot be made *in* her. Otherwise, the images represent the surface of Lucretius' pictures of reality, but they fail to represent, they deny, the feeling-tone of those pictures. 'Torrents' seems at first glance to be nothing more than a properly dynamic representation of how universes-in-motion look, but it comes to reverberate with the near hysteria that is created in the beholder when 'ruining' links up with 'the illimitable inane', a phrase whose denotation is properly Epicurean but whose connotation, empty, unreal, groundless, is sinister: the entire line is Tennyson at his uncanny-grandest. Why should Nature's eternal integration/disintegration of myriad universes – a doctrine he has been preaching throughout his poem, an idea that he thrills to, a fact that should *rid* him of the materials for bad dreams – why should it bother him, why should it have become one of his (new?) nightmares? Because this dream, like the two that follow it, manifest, in textbook style, 'the return of the repressed'. The poet of the *DRN* writes superbly of the destruction of the world. He thinks, in his conscious mind, that he believes what he says about what that destruction means. (It means nothing except that it teaches him how to acquire some measure of serenity, which will in turn allow him to enjoy reality as it is.) But at this moment, his mind wavering between its consciousness and its unconsciousness, the poet finds himself mistrustful of atomic truth and its gospel of pleasure. His belief is shaken: what his brute brain seems to believe is that the godless void and its atoms make up an entity that wants to devour him.

In his second dream the bloodshed in which Sulla drenched Italy becomes a rainstorm.

> And where it dash'd the reddening meadows sprang
> No dragon warriors from Cadmean teeth,
> For these I thought my dream would show to me,
> But girls, Hetairai, curious in their art,
> Hired animalisms, vile as those that made
> The mulberry-faced Dictator's orgies worse
> Than aught they fable of the quiet Gods.
> And hands they mixt, and yell'd and round me drove
> In narrowing circles ...

Two fears his philosophy had banished here return together, allied to undo his serenity. The truth of Epicurus had showed him how to free himself and others from the insane ambitions of Sulla and from the chaos they engender. Likewise, he had learned from the atomic truth how bestial lust can be tamed and serenity achieved, but now a swarm of whores (Hetairai), like trained and performing animals, creatures like those whom Sulla assembled for his filthy pleasures, surround and press themselves against him. The powerlessness of the truth that he had not only relied upon himself but that he also felt called upon to disseminate to others is now made clear to him. He has no defence against the wickedness of history and none, either, against the salacious urgencies that bubble inside him. (The specific details of Sulla's skin problems are mentioned in a passage from Plutarch's biography of him, one that also discusses his same-sexual attachments to post-adolescent male actors whom the Hetairai seem here to have displaced.) His wisdom, once again, is – so the deeper 'brute' brain that does not lie reveals to him – a sham.

In his third dream, the displacements and condensations are at once less elaborate and more intricate:

> Then, then, from utter gloom stood out the breasts,
> The breasts of Helen, and hoveringly a sword
> Now over and now under, now direct,

112

Pointed itself to pierce, but sank down shamed
At all that beauty; and as I stared, a fire,
The fire that left a roofless Ilion,
Shot out of them, and scorch'd me that I woke.

Sometimes a sword is only a sword perhaps. This one, however, confesses its true identity pretty clearly when it loses its erection. Furthermore, the pen is, for poets, mightier than the sword, it is their special style of potency. Helen and her flame-throwing breasts, then, continue the theme of repressed lust from the previous dream, but their beauty (and fatality) also signal the mythology that the atomist claims to have defabricated with atomic truth (that he wants to kill and cannot), and in particular they connote the poem of Lucretius' direct heir, Vergil's *Aeneid*, in Book 2 of which its hero, Aeneas, gets the chance to murder the woman whose beauty caused the destruction of his city; he is about to kill Helen of Sparta and Troy when his mother Venus intervenes. Whatever Tennyson's own problems with the Perverse Feminine may have been (Colley 90-1; Shaw 127-9), this surreal usurpation of the Vergilian scene re-emphasises the poet's neurotic failure to cure himself of the lust he wants to cure in others (Shrink, shrink thyself) and reveals that his (insane) poetic project, to usurp epic poetry for the sole purpose of propagating Epicurean dogma and thereby to 'kill' it along with the gods and heroes who sustain it, is a failure. (For this project in the *DRN*, see Gale 42-7, 153-7, 190-2, 229-33.) At the close of the third and climactic segment of his lustful dream, hero of his own counter-epic, the anguished poet wakes (and not from a Lucretian wet dream, *DRN* 5.1030ff.) to find himself impotent just when he has most need of his pen/penis/sword and suffers thereby a humiliating defeat, wounded by the flaming breasts of the Archetypal Whore.

Awake and anxious, Lucretius wonders if 'holy Venus' is punishing him for his blasphemies (against her and her fellow gods), despite the splendid praises he offered her in his 'rich prooemion'. If she is one of the real gods who 'Live the great life which all our greatest fain/ Would follow, centre'd in eternal calm', she cannot, of course, be angry with him. In any case, in his poem he was not really talking about her; instead, using metaphor, 'did I take/ That popular name of thine to shadow forth/ The all-generating powers and genial heat/ Of Nature.'

He notices that, disturbed by his horrid dreams and seeking for their cause, he has stumbled back into the old illusion and he tries to focus his thoughts on the gods as they are:

> The Gods, who haunt
> The lucid interspace of world and world,
> Where never creeps a cloud, or moves a wind,
> Nor ever falls the least white star of snow,
> Nor ever lowest roll of thunder moans,
> Nor sound of human sorrow mounts to mar
> Their sacred everlasting calm!

No one but Tennyson wrote sights and sounds like these, and they perfectly answer in English what the ancient poet had in mind. But this Lucretius is not satisfied with his orthodox meditation on deity and he begins to wonder how it is possible that gods who are made up of atoms are not 'dissoluble', do 'not follow the great law' like everything else. In this matter, as in all others, he has tried his hardest to follow Epicurus:

> I prest my footsteps into his, and meant
> Surely to lead my Memmius in a train
> Of flowery clauses onward to the proof
> That Gods there are, and deathless. Meant? I meant?
> I have forgotten what I meant: my mind
> Stumbles, and all my faculties are lamed.

Defeated in life, impotent as a poet, helpless despite (or because of) Epicurus, he is abandoned by the meaning of his poem, and his intentions for it are now as incomprehensible to him as the convolutions of his own mind in its shattering or as the world that dissolves beneath his feet.

Desperately, the poet looks up into the sky at 'another of our Gods, the Sun'. Memories of this god's mythological/poetical images drift, with a kind of solace through his mind (the sun 'slowly lifts/ His golden feet on those empurpled stairs/ That climb into the windy halls of heaven'). But the poet also thinks of the actual sun and how it looks down upon the faces of infants wailing at their birth and upon the faces

114

of dying men 'That fain would gaze upon him to the last' and upon the faces of the dead and those who mourn them. Perhaps half-remembering Dryden's memorable emphasis on the futility of birth in his Lucretian versions, Tennyson here links it with elegant images of death scenes: the sun which sustains life and lights it and cheers it, when robbed of its poetry, is utterly heedless of human experience and utterly ignorant of human suffering and human purpose: 'And me altho' his fire is on my face/ Blinding, he sees not, nor at all can tell/ Whether I mean this day to end myself'). This Lucretius can no longer be certain of what he previously *meant* to do (in his life, in his poem), but he is now groping to find what he *means* 'this day' to do. Plato says suicide is forbidden by the gods, but Epicurus knows better:

> ... he that holds
> The Gods are careless, wherefore need he care
> Greatly for them, nor rather plunge at once,
> Being troubled, wholly out of sight, and sink
> Past earthquake – ay, and gout and stone, that break
> Body toward death, and palsy, death-in-life,
> And wretched age –

This is an option that the Master in fact disapproved of, but his litany of physical infirmities incites the incipient (and crazed) apostate to disregard what the Master said on this matter (and others). When he continues his catalogue of the miseries that suicide would put an end to, we have more than an inkling of what disturbs him most about being alive. Lust (repressed again and again returned) caps the list:

> – and worst disease of all,
> These prodigies of myriad nakedness,
> And twisted shapes of lust, unspeakable,
> Abominable, strangers at my hearth
> Not welcome, harpies miring every dish,
> The phantom husks of something foully done,
> And fleeting thro' the boundless universe,
> And blasting the long quiet of my breast
> With animal heat and dire intensity!

At this point, perhaps we should recall that, in this narrative, as in the legend it is modelled on, this disruption of sanity is caused by a 'wicked broth' which 'confused the chemic labour of the blood'. Tennyson's Lucretius is perhaps innocent of his derelictions from orthodoxy; perhaps he is expressing nothing more, in his monologue, than his experience of his delusions while under the influence of the philtre. But, even allowing for the possibility that the philtre may be a malfunctioning aphrodisiac, it is also possible, even likely, that, on the *in vino veritas* principle, the drug is revealing what is actually in the poet's mind, what he has been attempting to hide or escape from by writing his poem.

Seen in this light, his writing the *DRN* would be (this is, after all, one of the functions of writing) his way of talking himself into what he would like to believe and talking his way out of what he wants to repress – or, as in the case of Helen of the lovely breasts – to kill. If that's the case, it hasn't worked. 'The boundless universe,' which was the cause both of his 'divine joy and shivering' and of 'the long quiet of my breast', is now transformed into a demonic phantasmagoria of countless shapes performing their lustful geometries, shitting on his food, corrupting the bright, pure universe (and his mind) with their (and his) bestial madness.

Bombarded by images that emanate from the objects of his illicit desire, he is maddened by myriad images of complex lubricities which represent, for all their plenitude, the same 'something foully done'. Epicurus reduces these multitudes to their common denominator (this is precisely what Lucretius does in Book 4, see particularly 1061-72): sex is sex and it's mostly in the head; if you're that horny, have a cold shower, jerk yourself off, hire yourself a girl or boy, order a slave to do his duty – then, forget it. But Tennyson's Lucretius, partly perhaps because he's a Christian (or becoming, in the world of Darwin, a post-Christian), can't do that. He broods; it festers: 'How should the mind, except it loved them, clasp/ These idols to herself'). They become, in their swarms, like a 'multitude' (a mob) that 'jam through the doors, and bear/ Their keepers down, and throng, their rags and they/ The basest, far into that council-hall/ Where sit the best and stateliest of the land!' Beast against Human, Mob against Rulers ('keepers'!), Lust ('animal heat') against Reason. The poem's original knew all about the mob, but he expected nothing better (in fact he

116

expected worse) from 'the keepers'. In these lines Tennyson erases his original's warnings about how those in power behave and, with a dazzling somersault from lust to anarchy ('their *rags*' betrays the degree of anxiety that fuels his gymnastics) stamps the hysteria of his heroic anti-hero with a contemporary mental snapshot: the brutal underclasses that, left unchecked, will invade that citadel of Reason, Parliament.

The distraught poet manages to tear his mind away from this dreadful image of the-centre-not-holding by turning it from the city to the country, to pristine Nature. He tries to see nature as it is, but instead he sees poetry, sees images of rustic Gods, which lead immediately to a stirring in the trees ('yon arbutus/ Totters; a noiseless riot underneath/ Strikes through the woods, sets all the tops quivering'), for this is the place of 'Nymph and Faun', and what his eye fixes on is a mountain nymph. 'How the sun delights,' cries the poet,

> To glance and shift about her slippery sides
> And rosy knees and supple roundedness,
> And budded bosom-peaks –

We have gathered, by now, that Tennyson's Lucretius is very definitely a breast man. But it isn't he alone who has spotted the 'budded bosom-peaks' (not to mention the knees and the curves). As she runs towards the poet (with a touch of Ovid to set her in motion?) 'before the rest' (of her sister nymphs), 'a satyr, a satyr, see, follows'. Shades of Mallarmé and Nijinsky! The poet reminds himself that such creatures do not exist ('him I proved impossible/ Twy-nature is no nature' = *DRN* 5.878-82, also 4.789f.), but the picture doesn't fade, 'he draws / Near and Nearer'. Close up, the poet can see that he is 'Beastlier than any phantom of his kind/ That ever butted his rough brother-brute/ For lust or lusty blood or provender.' He knows what the monster is after. 'I hate, abhor, spit, sicken at him.' Yes, because it takes one to know one. The nymph also detests him, and she rushes towards the poet, desperate to elude the brute: 'will she fling herself,/ Shameless upon me?' The poet can't have that happening. He cheers the satyr on: 'Catch her, goatfoot.' Then he begs the forest to overwhelm them and hide them from his sight. He wants the vision destroyed.

Again, in his despair, he calls out to the Gods. He knows that they are 'careless, yet, behold, to you/ From childly wont and ancient use I call.' The repressed has claimed him, so he speaks in the language of his childhood, the language of his fathers, the language he thought he had unlearned when he learned, from Epicurus, a new language for a new life. He says to the Gods:

> I thought I lived securely as yourselves –
> No lewdness, narrowing envy, monkey-spite,
> No madness of ambition, avarice, none:
> No larger feast than under plane or pine
> With neighbours laid along the grass, to take
> Only such cups as left us friendly-warm ...

The ideal Lucretian moment, the picnic with friends, all but hides the arrogance which might, in another poem, be the key to the poet's ruin: the poet of the *DRN* hardly imagined that his *voluptas* equalled or could equal that of the gods. The complacent arrogance of Tennyson's Lucretius betrays his failure, once again asserted, to accept, whole-heartedly, the doctrines of his Master. But that arrogance passes unnoticed by the speaker. He insists that in the blessedness of the picnic there was 'Nothing to mar the sober majesties/ Of settled, sweet, Epicurean life.' But to the speaker, now, it is not the delusions that Epicurus unmasked, but his picnics and his doctrines themselves, that seem delusive.

> But now it seems some unseen monster lays
> His vast and filthy hands upon my will,
> Wrenching it backward into his; and spoils
> My bliss in being ...

'Bliss in being' is a wonderful rendering of Lucretian *voluptas*. But it is 'the unseen monster' and 'his vast and filthy hands' and *his* 'will', not the speaker's will nor Lucretius' atomistic truth or his gospel of pleasure, that (we now see) control this poem. There is a sort of Gothic stench to this monster and the verses that incarnate him. But his evil is purer than that. He is not only the speaker's dark, secret self, spawn of 'the brute brain within the man's' (he is Darwin's child, born 1859;

118

Shaw 130), he is also 'an absence of being', he is 'unbeing' that devours being. And the 'bliss in being' that the monster 'spoiled'?

> ... and it was not great;
> For save when shutting reasons up in rhythm,
> Or Heliconian honey in living words,
> To make a truth less harsh, I often grew
> Tired of so much within our little life,
> Or of so little in our little life –
> Poor little life that toddles half an hour
> Crown'd with a flower or two, and there an end –

Writing the poem helped him endure his existence, telling pretty lies to sweeten harsh truths distracted him from thinking about how cluttered his life was – and how paltry, how brief, how meaningless, how boring. (Baudelaire decadent? Swinburne decadent?) Being an Epicurean helped this Lucretius a little, then, being an Epicurean poet helped a little more, but:

> ... since the nobler pleasure seems to fade,
> Why should I, beastlike as I find myself,
> Not manlike end myself?

Again he forgets the Epicurean dislike of suicide and opts for the solution that Stoics and noble Romans agree on. It was noble Romans who won for Rome the grandeur that is now fading like 'the nobler pleasure' of Epicurus. Among them was one whose name recalls his own: Lucretia's blood drove out the bad kings and established the Commonwealth which now 'breaks/ As I am breaking now!'

It is an extremely un-Epicurean finish for the poster-boy for Epicureanism. His final identification with the Republic and *Romanitas* belies his identity as a follower of (and spokesman for) the Master. So, in this poem, Lucretius was a fraud, and maybe Epicurus was too. We can blame it on the aphrodisiac, of course, or we can suggest that the poem gestures towards indeterminacy: maybe the aphrodisiac is talking, or maybe it triggers a revelation of the speaker's true shallowness – and the true worthlessness of the philosophy he and his poem espouse. But there is too much in the way of 'lucid intervals' in the poem for it to represent a mind in headlong ruin, wholly controlled by fatal drugs. His reason observes his madness too keenly and judges it too sternly for us to suppose that Mr Hyde seizes the microphone permanently.

Furthermore, the poem's close is spoken by a reasonable and noble Roman:

> And therefore now
> Let her, that is the womb and tomb of all,
> Great Nature, take, and forcing far apart
> Those blind beginnings that have made me man
> Dash them anew together at her will
> Through all her cycles – into man once more,
> Or beast or bird or fish, or opulent flower.

One last glimpse of atomistic truth intrudes upon this Roman suicide. He remembers how things break apart and then recombine, everywhere, always, in fresh new forms, but that vision itself crumbles (brilliantly) into fragments. Tennyson refashions the Lucretian explosion of this (and every) planet when: 'cosmic order everywhere/ Shatter'd into one earthquake in one day/ Cracks all to pieces.' Perhaps soon 'momentary man/ Shall seem no more a something to himself ', and 'his hopes and hates, his homes and fanes/ And even his bones' will disappear 'Vanishing, atom and void, atom and void/ Into the unseen forever.' Soon or late, that day, that hour, will come. But until then, and as long as 'momentary man' seems 'something to himself ', as long as he is not 'tired of so much within our little life,/ Or of so little in our little life', so long as he finds or tries to find his life worth living (unlike the speaker whose pretty lies deceive him), until the planet explodes, 'My golden work in which I told a truth ... Shall stand: ay, surely: then it fails at last/ And perishes as I must.' The truth he told (which 'plucks/ The mortal soul from out immortal hell') is that the hell of the poets does not exist (but why and how is that hell here 'immortal'?). Was that the only truth he told? Here, at the end of his life and of his poem, the only teaching of the Master that he seems to credit, the only verse he wrote about those teachings that he cares to endorse (when he describes his 'work' as 'golden', is he being ironic?), is the doctrine of the soul's mortality (and hell's unreality). His vision of the dynamic of the

120

destruction and creation of the infinite worlds reduces itself to this world and its destruction (and his poem's destruction: that's how poets think, of course, since their immortality and that of their poems are identical, but one doubts it's the way the real poet of the real *DRN* is likely to have thought).

Just before he ends his monologue and drives 'the knife into his side', he addresses his final words to 'Thou,/ Passionless bride, divine Tranquillity.' He tells this goddess that she is 'Yearn'd after by the wisest of the wise,/ Who fail to find thee, being as thou art/ Without one pleasure or without one pain.' Nevertheless, he assures her that he will find her in death, wooing her 'roughly, for thou carest not/ How roughly men may woo thee so they win –/ Thus – thus: the soul flies out and dies in the air.' 'Thus – thus': here he stabs himself to death and so embraces in oblivion the Tranquillity that eluded him in life. Here, in effect, the poem ends, although poor Lucilia, having heard him rage and topple over, rushes in, shrieking with self-recriminations: she has failed in her duty to him, she has been a poor excuse for The Angel in the House. The dying Lucretius is clasped in her arms, is kissed by her, and, in a tender moment of Christian charity (and bathos), he forgives her: 'Care not thou!' he murmurs, 'Thy duty! What is duty? Fare thee well.' Hollywood, eat your heart out.

But to return to the poem's real closure: in his address to Tranquillity, Tennyson's Lucretius reveals the central, fatal mistake he has been making all along, one that generates all his failure as an atomic hedonist, one that the poet of the *DRN* could never make: he thinks of his (passionless) tranquillity as being 'without one pleasure and without one pain'. Epicurean happiness consists in lacking bodily pain and lacking mental pain that would distract one both from pleasant sensations and from pleasant thoughts. Here is the core of Lucretius' version of tranquillity: 'O joyless hearts of men! O minds without vision! How dark and dangerous the life in which this tiny span is lived away! Do you not see that nature is barking for two things only, a body free from pain and a mind released from worry and fear for the enjoyment of pleasurable sensations?' (*DRN* 2.14-19). Just as Tennyson's poet, in his last representation of our planet's final cataclysm, fails to remember that this 'ending' is part of a universal and eternal process of creation and destruction and fails to understand that this event is part of the truth that – however paradoxically – brings with it *quaedam divina voluptas atque horror,* so he equates an empty body-mind, a dead body-mind, with tranquillity, which, for Lucretius seems rather to be the part of the bodily-mental process that occurs just after the banishment of physical and mental pains when one's pure enjoyment of the world and of one's body-mind-in-the-world begins; I suppose one could even say that there is almost no point in making such a distinction between this tranquillity and this enjoyment of absent-pain and present-pleasure, so enmeshed is the one process with the other. Tennyson's poet, in short, is a failed Epicurean. He has some of the right words, but all the wrong music; he is ignorant or forgetful of first Epicurean principles to the point that one is tempted to think of him as an imposter. What is this poem about?

In an astute summation of its central themes, Kalika Ranjan Chatterjee (67) suggests that the poem 'is a warning against the revival of the Lucretian philosophy, with its materialism, its naturalism, and its secularism ... To him [Tennyson], the Atomism of Lucretius, with its mechanical conception of cosmic operation, is a philosophy of pessimism and despair, of defeat and social destruction.' This reading of the poem does not take into account its tangled and pervasive eroticism, nor does it sufficiently allow for a conflicted Tennyson who perhaps felt himself attracted to the liberation that Lucretius offers but could not bring himself to accept it. Nevertheless Chatterjee's version helps us see why it is that Tennyson might have written (not with his conscious mind alone) this ferocious (and admiring) cartoon. He had got hold of Munro's edition, he heard in it echoes of the Vergil that he loved, he began to surrender to the poem's amazing sights and sounds, he was enchanted and terrified by the truths about (his) sexuality that he found there, he began to be obsessed with the poem, its dark moods and its exaltations, he began to write that obsession into a poem.

Both for its incomparable technique and for its extraordinary emotional propulsion this is, until just its final verses, a magnificent poem (if you don't believe me, make the experiment of reading it out loud – and don't be afraid to ham it up). Not a little of the poem's emotive power (which stretches and is enhanced by its infallible technical equipment) derives from the fact that the *DRN* ended by terrifying Tennyson. His sexuality, his politics, his theology, his position as a producer of culture – all these were called into question by a voice whose extraordinary power he recognised. His writing 'Lucretius' was his way of escaping both Lucretius and the anxieties that his milieu and moment inflicted on him. He may have thought of the poem as being, as in a sense it is, a homage to Lucretius, but what he ended with was a new version of Anti-Lucretius, the melancholy suicide who could not be saved by the philosophy that he preached. And that poem, because it was Tennyson who wrote it, and because it was a very beautiful and very powerful poem, became, in the English-speaking world, through its century and for half of the century that followed it, a touchstone for the reading of the *DRN*. When educated people still read Tennyson, this version of the melancholiac was as real to them as Hamlet or Macbeth or Ahab or Gatsby. The cartoon was now the reality.

Who's afraid of Titus Lucretius Carus?

Back across the channel, 1859 (while Arnold is discovering melancholy in Lucretius, while Darwin is dawning): M. Patin is lecturing his students at the Académie Française, mapping out the ground he intends to cover with them in their 1859-1860 course. Together, they will read Books 5 and 6 of the *DRN*. What he plans to focus on are the frequent moments in the poem when 'Lucretius, without knowing it, is actually sympathetic with what he fights against with so much conviction, with such passion, is actually drawn to what he prides himself in having conquered and destroyed': Creationism, Providence, the Immortality of the Human Soul, The Swerve of Free Will, etc., etc. (Patin 118).

In this introductory lecture, Patin must limit himself to leafing through 'this huge poem' and picking out signal examples of 'its involuntary contradictions', its silent self-refutations, and, in particular, its bizarre, atheistic theology (118). What this method will reveal is a pervasive tension between the poet's ubiquitous (and obsessive) demystifications of religion and his inconsistent and ardent recourse to religious imagery and religious ideas (Venus, the Muse, Magna Mater, Mother Earth, Nature the Creator, Nature the Sustainer, Divina Voluptas). The theory behind this analysis of hidden tensions is dear to the French heart: it is the Wizard of Oz exposed by Toto, it is what happens in Montaigne and Rabelais as well as in Lucien Goldmann, in Barthes, in Macherey, in Derrida (and I have just availed myself of it in reading Tennyson). Patin finds what self-decon-structs the *DRN* in Polignac's poem, at the point where the Cardinal reminds the godless materialist that he cannot efface the footprints of the god he flees from (127). Lucretius keeps saying that creation is the result of a blind but lucky clash of atoms, but he quickly finds himself talking about how the atoms move according to procedures, treaties, laws, he has to call on Nature that creates and Nature that 'steers the ship'; this is 'the reef upon which is wrecked the irreligious system he has fashioned with such persuasive conviction' (120). What his poem actually reveals, then, is a profound but 'involuntary spirituality' (132), a poet who, 'through some fatal mistake, turned away from his true path', since 'by nature, he was called towards another philosophi-cal system' (135). (A proto-Christian Stoic?) In any case, long before his sublime and ravishing poem incited Polignac to pick up his pen in defence of the Faith, it was Lucretius himself 'so to speak, who was the first Anti-Lucretius' (118).

Just over a decade later, in 1869, Constant Martha published, in his book on Lucretius, a chapter titled 'Tristesse du Système'. He begins by remarking that 'nowadays it's the fashion to applaud poets for being depressed and we think of melancholy as poetry's greatest charm' (Martha 315). Which is perhaps why certain people (he doesn't men-tion Patin by name) have started describing Lucretius as a 'sceptic who suffers from his scepticism, who has fallen prey to anxiety occasioned by his doubt, who longs for truths that his doctrines cannot give him, one who feels himself robbed of his childhood faith and who, though without being exactly able to feel regret for losses he can't admit to, nevertheless suffers the disturbances of a rational mind that is unsat-isfied by what it has embraced'. Deconstruction (which occurs when the speaker of a poem cannot play by the rules of the game that he himself has laid down for himself) is not Martha's cup of tea. He begs to differ. There is no point in Epicurean doctrine where Lucretius does not feel utterly at home. In fact, in the entire history of philsophy Martha doubts that 'there could be found another example of a convic-tion so complete, of a faith so entire, of an attachment to the Word of the Master so obstinate' (315-16). What's all the fuss about then? 'It's not the poet who is sad ... the sadness is in the system itself.' What Patin and his cohorts can't understand is that Lucretius fails to be a happy hedonist not because he is susceptible to anxiety attacks (induced or not by wifely chemicals) but because the basic tenets of the sect he belongs to are by their very nature melancholy.

Patin believes the most cursory comparison with the essence of Stoicism instantly demonstrates Epicureanism's intrinsic *tristesse*. The Stoics recognise the manifest order of nature. They also 'believe in Providence and insist that physical pain is often nothing more than illusion, or mere necessity, or an opportunity for giving the zeal and virtue of Man a chance to show its mettle' (318-19). Epictetus, in Sylvester Stallone mode, is quoted praying to Jupiter to send him trials to test him (what would Hercules have been without those nasty beasts to slaughter?), and he reviles the wretched hedonists who 'sit there, trembling, whining. It is your spinelessness that has turned you into impious fools' (319). It is 'soft Epicureanism that, wanting nature to prepare for it a bed of repose, found God's Law of Labour oppressive and unjust'. To these snivelling cowards the world seems in steady decline. So, when they turn their gaze from earth to heaven, like Pascal, they are devastated by their insignificance, their 'nothingness compared with the immensity of space and with eternity'. Such thoughts 'are not sad in themselves, or rather, they have only the sadness that accords with a severe grandeur' (325-6). (On 316, when first comparing the Lucretian vision with Pascal's, he had remarked that the immensity of nature and the great mysteries of the world induced in both writers 'huge and lofty thoughts, filled with melancholy'.) Stoics (again) would not find themselves in a funk when staring out into the heavens since they know that, however small man's place in the universe may be, he nevertheless carries within him part of the Universal Spirit. People who think of themselves as clods or ragbags formed by a lucky (or luckless) clash of atoms cannot be expected to feel that way, and they will doubtless become despondent. They don't believe in Order or Providence or Courage or Justice. What do they believe in?

They believe in a 'happy apathy, which is the goal and the price of their wisdom. Nothing troubles the Epicurean, nothing surprises him, nothing moves him ... but he is finally smothered in the tight folds of his narrow doctrine. Boredom enters into the soul that the passions have deserted' (334). (Has Martha been sneaking a look at Baudelaire?) 'The uniform spectacle of [this dull] world, of which he is the lazy observer, wearies him and irritates him.' How greatly an ardent spirit like Lucretius' might have been affected by these heavy doses of this stale air, Martha cannot pretend to know, but he thinks we might hazard a guess by looking at 'the veil of mourning that covers his poetry' (335). How could it be otherwise? Wonderful though Epicurus' attack on superstition might be, beneficial though it has been, it went 'beyond its goal' when he refused to recognise the omnipotence of true divinity and, losing that, consigned his disciples 'to intellectual stumbling and vacillation and sometimes to sadness'. Martha's closing paragraphs elaborate on that confusion and that grief. Though man and the world may be delivered (in the poem) from the 'hated power of the gods', 'a nameless and hidden power remains behind to turn human grandeur upside down' (330). Lucretius may say he believes only in chance, but he ends up 'ascribing providence and beneficence and even anger to an omnipotent nature'. He depicts the disorders of turbulent heaven, but in 'its astonishing and mysterious regularity' he is dismayed to see what seems to be 'the hand of God'. Like Pascal, his 'imagination seems still haunted by the things which he attacks and whose existence he denies' (Pascal's by Reason, his, by the gods).

Despite his claim of opposition to Patin, Martha shares his predecessor's essential perspective when he sets out to analyse what he takes to be Lucretius' ineradicable need of transcendence and what he believes to be the necessary and fundamental despair of those who claim to interpret and celebrate a world without providence to guide it. Is Lucretius a sad man in a happy system? Or is he someone searching for happiness whom a sad system saddens? Both these readings of the poem grow from the same soil. In 1717, Marchetti's Italian translation of the *DRN* was printed in London (three years after its author's death); the next year, in Rome, it was put on the Index. Thirty years later there appeared Polignac's poem. A little over two decades later (1770, about the time of Diderot's *Dream* and Voltaire's *Memmius*) appeared Holbach's scandalous and Lucretian *Système de la nature*. Materialism, partly in the guise of a great ancient Latin poem, had taken firm root in French culture. After the Revolution this dangerous book, this famous and powerful poem, became more and more available, in more translations, and more and more people were reading it. The other classics could be baptised or truncated or ignored. This one, with its superb hymns to the truth of science and materialism, could not. Christians needed to find ways of defending the truths of the Church, they needed to find ways of responding to free thinkers, to people like J.B.S. de Pongerville, who himself had translated the *DRN* (in 1823) and who closed his entry on Lucretius in the *Dictionnaire de la Conversation et de la Lecture* (1856) with these words: 'The veil of prejudice that has for so long been stretched across the beauties of the poem is now lifted.' Other good poets do their thing, he says, and come and go. But Lucretius, 'though he sometimes fails as a natural scientist, as a philosophical poet is always infallible, and no other poet has flown higher in the heavens of intellect or stayed there longer .... Nature has never looked as sublime as it does when we see it through the eyes of Lucretius.' Thus, he 'remains, in his supremacy, always new, like nature, of which he is the interpreter'.

Since the Index hadn't done the job, Patin and Martha and their readers tried deconstruction: they transformed Lucretius into his anti-self, made him unsay what he really said and say what he never said. That way he was no longer a peril, that way he was safe. Now people could read him without being infected. Or – just as good or better – they did not have to bother reading him, no matter how famous he was, no matter how beautiful the Latin or exquisite his images, because he was confused and confusing, because he was down in the dumps himself and reading him put you down there with him. And who needs that?

*

Back across the channel (again), a similar tale was playing itself out in a rather different way. For a masterly account of its manifold complexities, the reader should go to Frank Turner's splendid essay, 'Lucretius Among the Victorians'; I limit myself here chiefly to its aftermath wherein Lucretius is declawed and defanged and thus rendered suitable for inclusion among the great books that are set for examinations. At the beginning of the century, in his introduction to his translation (1806) of the *DRN*, Thomas Busby had stipulated on what terms the godless materialist would be allowed to survive as an exemplary genteel humanist (and great poet):

The scholar who should receive Lucretius for his religious guide, would be deemed insane; and he who in the present advanced state of science should study him for a new insight into the occult principles of nature, would have little credit with us for his wisdom; but he who takes up his poem with a view to refined and elegant gratification; to indulge the raptures of poetry; to enjoy the most striking and luxurious pictures of nature; to collect rules for a moral and happy life; or with ingenious curiosity to observe the eccentricities to which the brightest mind, unaided by divine illumination, is ever liable, will receive a rich and ample compensation for the time he devotes to its perusal. (xi)

(For Byron's low opinion of Busby's translation, see his Journal for 17 November 1813.) In H.A.J. Munro's introduction to his edition to the *DRN* (Fourth Edition, 1893) we find, as though nothing had happened since Busby published his expensive – and still beautiful to see and touch – two-volume translation:

To Lucretius the truth of his philosophy was all-important: to this the graces of his poetry were made altogether subordinate. To us on the other hand the truth or falsehood of his system is of exceedingly little concern except in so far as it is thereby rendered a better or worse vehicle for conveying the beauties of his language and the graces of his poetical conceptions. (5)

For Busby, the truths that impassioned the poet's mind are insane, to Munro, they are irrelevant; they agree that it is poetic beauty that matters (though Busby wants also to squeeze some morality out of that beauty and he wants to offer the poet's hybris as a cautionary tale). Looking at the basic agreement of the two comments, you would think that nothing much had happened to the reception of Lucretius from the beginning of the century to its end. But it had. By the beginning of the twentieth century the blasphemer who had worried Busby has vanished as though he had never been. What's left of him can be used as a junkyard where historians of ancient philosophy try to find some of the many missing pieces of their puzzle (does he represent Epicurus accurately or is he just an upstart Roman groupie who muddies the purities of the Grecian argument?). Or the philologists can take him up tenderly (noble, sad, revered) and (it is Sellar's model, pp. 107-9 above) try to alleviate parental concern or deflect what may be left of priestly anxiety (is he an atheist? is he like Tennyson's lunatic?) by trotting out Dryden's pabulum, or by trying to read the *DRN* as if Tennyson had never written his version of it (or by reading his version as one that endorsed the Latin poet's huge nobility: for an atheist, self-slaughter is the gentleman's way out, the only decent thing to do). But the debate is essentially over, and the war is won. Atomist or not, the ancient materialist is now harmless.

This is how that came about. Six years after Tennyson published his poem, John Tyndall, then President of the British Association for the Advancement of Science, chose to spotlight Epicurus and Lucretius in his presidential address ('The Belfast Address', 1874; vol 2). In his representation of the poet's hostility to ancient Roman theology, Tyndall drily reveals his own to the theology of his day: 'his object, like that of his great forerunner, is the destruction of superstition; and considering that men in his day trembled before every natural event as a direct monition from the gods, and that everlasting torture was also in prospect, the freedom aimed at by Lucretius might be deemed a positive good' (142). He then proceeds to offer a brief, very sympathetic and rather lyrical description of Lucretius' version of atomism, which leads him to praise the poet's 'strong scientific imagination'. His peroration to this first section of his speech leaves no doubt about his admiration for the vision Lucretius offers (of which hatred of theology is part and parcel) and about his desire to affirm its affinities with the science which he practices:

Far beyond the limits of our visible world are to be found atoms innumerable, which have never been united to form bodies, or which, if once united, have been again dispersed – falling silently through immeasurable intervals of time and space ... Above us, below us, beside us, there are worlds without end; and this, when considered, must dissipate every thought of the deflection of the universe by gods. The worlds come and go, attracting new atoms out of limitless space, or dispersing their own particles. The reputed death of Lucretius, which forms the basis of Mr. Tennyson's noble poem, is in strict accordance with his philosophy, which was severe and pure. (144-5)

The Lucretian vision of atoms and the void that Tyndall rehearses here is one that he recognises almost as his own. This vision of atomic reality fills Tyndall with admiration and compels his assent. Such a reality and such a world do not need god(s). The intellectual strength and the unpersuadable irreligiosity are interdependent and they validate one another. As for the silly gossip about his death, invented by the pious to demonise him, well – Tennyson's 'noble poem' has explained all that: he had come through the madness, in death as in life and as in his poem, he was 'severe and pure'. Splendour! It all cohered.

The Christians began dancing in the streets. On a silver platter Tyndall had handed them his head and Lucretius' as well (Turner 336-8). If, as Tyndall claimed, modern findings on the nature of reality were adumbrated by Lucretius, then, since it was obvious that very much of what he had to say was downright wrong or at best imprecise, that meant that the moderns who claimed kinship with him were also mistaken in their loud opinions. The defenders of Providence and Creation also pointed out (a dim memory from Polignac?) that Lucretius had been attacking (rightly) evil pagan gods (thus doing God's work by eradicating the chief obstacles to early Christian worship). Thus it was that (in Turner's words, 338) 'Lucretius ... became a pawn in the struggle for cultural domination between men of science and men of religion.' As the skirmishes continued over the next decade, men of science would gradually distance themselves from Tyndall's Lucretius and would increasingly stress the differences between their projects and that of the ancients (including Lucretius). In the end, Lucretius has been handed over to the Academy's museum of texts (from which Homer and Plato and Greek Tragedy and Thucydides were just then escaping, back into the real world and its various relevances).

By now, Lucretius is useless baggage to the scientists. If they happen to be theists or deists, he offers nothing much they want. If they are some variety of materialist, they have other and better and fresher fish to fry. We aren't surprised to find the great physicist, William Thomson, Baron Kelvin of Largs (1824-1907) saying, in a letter to a niece at Christmas, 1895: 'I have been reading Lucretius much helped by Munro's translation, and trying hard on my own to make something of the clash of atoms, but with little success' (Thompson 2.952-3) Only a few years later, in 1903, we find Lord

4. The Anti-Lucretius Himself

Kelvin defending himself against irate Christians who are dissatisfied by his timid affirmation of 'a creative and directive power' and displeased with his neglect of 'the propositions of the Apostle's Creed' (1101); he takes refuge in the authority of another deist, 'Cicero, editor of Lucretius' who 'denied that men and plants and animals could have come into existence by a fortuitous concourse of atoms ... If you think strongly enough you will be forced by science to believe in God, which is the foundation of all religion. You will find science not antagonistic to Religion', 1098-9). Just after Victoria's century ended, Cicero wins the day against his old opponent and his godless yet lucky collision of atoms.

He fares no better with scientists and scientific philosophers in the next century. In 1923, Einstein writes a blandly condescending page-and-a-half introduction to Hermann Diels' German translation of the *DRN*: through this poet's eyes, he says, we see how someone might imagine the world who had 'a flair for scientific speculation, who was gifted with lively thoughts and feelings and with intellectual independence, but who had no inkling of the results of modern scientific research – the sort of knowledge we nowadays provide our children with'. He is touched by the poet's reverence for Epicurus and for things Greek. 1939 finds Bertrand Russell in Los Angeles, writing to Robert Trevelyan for a favour. His eldest son, John, 'has a passion for Latin, especially Lucretius; unfortunately your Lucretius is stored in Oxford with the rest of my books' (*Autobiography 1914-1944*, 381; by 'your' he means Trevelyan's translations of selected passages). Trevelyan sends the volume to John (382) and is thanked by Russell ('John was *most* grateful for Lucretius', 384). Six years later, in his *A History of Western Philosophy*, Russell would give Lucretius the *coup de grace*: '... to the Roman aristocrat who stood aside from politics, and cared nothing for the scramble for power and plunder, the course of events [the ruin of the Republic] must have been profoundly discouraging. When to this was added *the affliction of recurrent insanity*, it is not to be wondered at that Lucretius accepted the hope of non-existence as a deliverance' (251; the italics are mine). Poor melancholy bastard.

His claims as a serious thinker demolished, Lucretius could finally be released from his duties as icon or shuttlecock or lightning rod in the Culture Wars that took place just before modernity began naming itself. He could be safely readmitted to the canon. Santayana, in his widely read *Three Philosophical Poets*, dismisses the apocryphal tattle about love-philtres and madness and suicide. These stories provide 'too edifying an end to an atheist and Epicurean not to be suspected' (19). Still – he wavers: 'If anything lends colour to the story it is a certain consonance which we may feel between its tragic incidents and the genius of the poet as revealed in his work, where we find *a strange scorn of love, a strange vehemence, and a high melancholy*' (the italics are mine). There it is again, the M word! 'It is,' continues Santayana, 'by no means incredible that the author of such a poem should have been at some time the slave of a pathological passion, that his vehemence and inspiration should have passed into mania, and that he should have taken his own life' (19-20). Sounds bad for Lucretius, but Santayana decides to have his cake and eat it too: 'But the untrustworthy authority of St Jerome cannot assure whether what he repeats is a tradition founded on fact or an ingenious fiction.' Nevertheless, this is a great poem, the work of 'a virile, practical intelligence', which grasps 'the prodigious mechanism' that 'produces life and often fosters it, yet as often makes it difficult and condemns it to extinction' (25). This is 'a truth with a melancholy side; but being a truth, it satisfies and exalts the rational mind, that craves truth as truth, whether it be sad or comforting ...'. Allegorically speaking, this mechanism can be called Nature, 'who destroys to create and creates to destroy, her interest being ... not in particular things, nor in their continuance, but solely in the movement that underlies them, in the flux of substance beneath' (43). Gazing at this, 'the philosopher is at the top of the wave, he is the foam in the rolling tempest; and as the wave must have risen before he bursts into being, all that he lives to witness is the fall of the wave. The decadence of all he lives by is the only prospect before him; his whole philosophy must be a prophecy of death ... Therefore, Lucretius, who is nothing if not honest, is possessed by a profound melancholy' (44).

Santayana's passionate admiration for various things about the poet and his poem can be found in his autobiography, *Persons and Places* (MIT Press, 1986, pp. 230, 538, 540, 622); but the finished portrait he offers us in the influential earlier volume is a peculiar amalgam of the various negative portraits we have seen in this chapter. In this version, Lucretius is a serious philosopher, but the (melancholy) truth he found is less important somehow than the sad worldview that has come to encrust it. It is this version of Lucretius, an extraordinary composite of various versions of his 'despair', that would persist, in strong forms or in weak, throughout the twentieth century. By and large, too many readings of the poem (its readers were now mostly in Academe) continued to be tinged with the sad legend of the saddest pagan who had cut himself off from cosmic comfort and paid the price for it both in this life and in the centuries that followed his death (Dalzell 1982, 214-15, 229 and 1998, 41-3; Jenkyns 234, 285-6; see also Bollack 128-45; Bradley 317-18, 321-2; Bright 628-32; Kinskey 127-30; Salem 244-6; Toohey 93-4, 103-8).

5

Wizards in Bondage

Oppenheimer was brilliant. But, like so many of those scientists, he needed someone with a strong character to manage him.

General Leslie Groves (Lamont 308)

By the close of the twentieth century Lucretius had become, essentially, a cherished preserve of students of Graeco-Roman literature and civilisation. He had his place, of course, among the Great Books and in various college survey courses. But he no longer had any share in the century's religious or cultural or ethical debates. He had had his day and had his say. That Christians and other believers should no longer bother with Lucretian blasphemies is prefectly understandable: they had evolutionists and Big-Bang cosmologists to worry about. But scientists, people whose worldviews were steeped in the truths of modern science, why should they not be interested in an ancient voice that proffered them, despite its huge scientific errors (Weinberg 169-71), a vision of the world that was, metaphysically and morally, exactly compatible with the vision of the world they had been constructing, decade after decade, as new observables and non-observables kept spilling into their nets? Was he saying what not a few of them, for various reasons, didn't want to hear?

There's no use in my hugging my cards to my chest. Let me fling them face up on the table. As a belletristic schoolmaster, as an innumerate and a scientific illiterate – a neo-Luddite I am not, convinced as I am that my kind is, *au fond*, a species of technological beast – I have no warrant whatever for what I'm going to say in this chapter. But I'm going to say it anyway. I think that some scientists, of both the theoretical and the practical varieties, might be wary of the *DRN*, if and when they chance on it, because its radical, in-your-face materialism ill accords with spiritual or cosmological hopes they hold dear (see McGinn 78-9 and 119-23 on the pitfalls of this style of cosmology; see also Weinberg 244-57). I think, too, that some scientists of a practical bent may be offended (or perhaps made ashamed?) by what Lucretius' calculus of pleasure has to say about their morals, values, and priorities. Looked at from Lucretius' perspective, both the scientist who relapses into a search for cosmic comfort and the scientist who refuses to help minimise suffering are wasting their brains and energies on new superstitions or, even worse, on the invention of unneeded, sometimes deadly, contraptions. I'm hardly suggesting that reading Lucretius will save the world or protect it from invasions by new generations of technomystics or fabricators of fatal progress. But I think it's worth pondering what these professions look like when bathed in Lucretian light, what help his poem might be able to offer us in our efforts to reconstruct the idea of science and of the world it has, in recent centuries, for worse and for better, remade.

Jodie Foster meets maybe God

The blurb on the back of the paperback of Carl Sagan's *Contact* (New York 1986) tells us that 'In December 1999, a multinational team journeys out to the stars, to the most awesome encounter in human history. Who – or what – is out there? In *Cosmos* Carl Sagan explained the universe. In *Contact*, he predicts its future – and our own.' In the movie version of the novel (1997), Jodie Foster travels 30,000 light years away from her planet all by herself (for purposes of dramatic economy and of spotlighting Foster, the film writers reduce the team from five multinationals to one white and feisty feminist; for my own purposes, economy among them, I make free to move back and forth from the movie to the novel). Sagan's heroine, Ellie Arroway, a SETI (Search for Extraterrestrial Intelligence) scientist, experiences enormous difficulties in securing funding for her projects and in warding off various governmental imbeciles from stealing her projects or ruining them. After many obstacles, she gets abundant financial backing from a very rich recluse (he is part Captain Nemo, part Howard Hughes) and is finally successful in making contact with intelligent beings *out there*. Having had some initial intergalactic chitchat with them, she decodes an intricate message they send her which supplies her with the recipe for a spaceship capable of transporting her over a distance of 30,000 light years from earth. So, having built the space-

136

craft and having womanfully faced more bureaucratic horrors (for the film's very PC gender sermons, see Davidson 405-9), she blasts off from earth and reaches her heavenly destination.

What she encounters there is, in fact, her father (or some kind of simulacrum of him) who explains to her a great deal of how the universe works (perhaps there is some dim intertextual linkage here, by way of type-scene, with Cicero's *Dream of Scipio*?). Her father had died when she was just a girl, but not before giving her scientific inclinations, good feminist father that he was, the strongest possible support. We are never entirely sure who or what the creature or apparition, 'disguised as her father' (I quote now from the novel, 361), might be, but we are certainly clear on one thing: since her father died she has been listening for messages from outer space and when she hears them and, at their bidding, goes to them, what she finds is something like her father (now revealed to be, in some manner, immortal) or something like the Voice of the Father. In any case, this entity reveals to her as much of the truth of the universe as she can begin to comprehend. He or it is a messenger of unimaginable realities, of truths that will someday be revealed in their totality, of the great togetherness of everything, of something beyond human reason, of something that is or might well be – divine. But if this father-figure is coy about his exact ontological status, it is a little more forthcoming about a certain 'hierarchy of beings.' Ellie decides that this hierarchy is 'on a scale she had not imagined. But the Earth had a place, a significant place in that hierarchy.' Otherwise, she reasons, 'they would not have gone to all this trouble for nothing' (365). 'They' seem to resemble something like the Head Engineers of the Universe, whose task, the cultivation and reconstruction of the universe, has just been described (364-5), and 'they' would not have bothered to get in touch with earth and, specifically, with Ellie unless Earth and she, her father's daughter (Father in Heaven), had a Mission to perform, for the good of the Universe.

Contact works pretty well as a film by virtue of its snazzy special effects and a bravura performance by Foster, whose ferocious conviction, her hallmark, distracts viewers from the tale's lush sentimentality. When I put her charisma and the film's fetching visuals aside, what I'm left with is a bizarre chunk of sci-fi theology wherein a genuine passion for scientific truth finds itself fused with conventional aesthetic appreciation of galactic wonders and with what amounts to mystical technology (Campbell 258-60). In the novel what is best described as a sort of mathematical theology, one which movie-mimesis can't do much with, is much in evidence (for the film's ambiguous theology, see Davidson 350, 377-8, 404-5, 409-11). Mathematics are the language of science, and they are, in Sagan's universe, also something like its god. Numbers are eternal. They may or may not be creational and providential as well, but in any case they need (or get) the help of ubiquitous and apparently immortal Engineers who perfect the work of creation, constantly redesigning it, constantly promoting and sustaining its eternal evolution (Hegel, anyone?). As the fatherly semblance describes it, when Ellie asks him to explain what he means by cultivation,

> 'the problem is that the universe is expanding, and there's not enough matter in it to stop the expansion. After a while, no new galaxies, no new stars, no new planets, no newly arisen lifeforms – just the same old crowd. Everything's getting run down. It'll be boring. So in Cygnus A we're testing out the technology to make something new. You might call it an experiment in urban renewal. (364)

No, let's call it an experiment in universal renewal or divine renewal. Lucky Ellie! In pursuing voices from outer space, she has not only stumbled upon cosmic comfort of a personal kind (an intimation of immortality, in any case, a reunion with her father in heaven), but has also glimpsed (and no longer merely through a telescope darkly) the theological nature of the scientific enterprise, one in which intellectual love of numbers is intricately, not to say divinely, enmeshed with the practical applications of the truths which that love reveals. If she (and Sagan) needed any justification for their love affair with outer space (Ellie's earthly love affair with Matthew McConaughey is cute but not crucial to her pilgrimage and its progress), if the Mission of Science in the Universe needed more validation, the encounter with Father more than provides it. Sagan's novel and movie (and much else that he wrote and said) remythify some of the basic superstitions that the Lucretian perspective defabricates, and they remystify questions about the uses of science that need (as the calculus of pleasure and Lucretius' version of atomic truth show) urgent and total reformulation.

Sagan was a valiant warrior for the environment and for nuclear responsibility, but there was another, dimmer strain to his sensibility. His attractive fervour for the beauty and truth of Science often propelled him into terrain where he lost sight of the limits of science, of its need *constantly* to rethink and reorder its priorities and obligations. In his 1994 book, *Pale Blue Dot: A Vision of the Human Future in Space*, he asks himself the daunting question: 'Can we, who have made such a mess of this world, be trusted with others?' (348). He decides that we can. The stratagems we devise in order to clean up our birthplace can then be used as we venture into the universe to 'terraform' other planets ('terraforming' is a term coined in 1942; it means 'making other planets earthlike' and thus habitable by earthlings). Not long before this vote of confidence he had reluctantly admitted that 'some limits might have to be set on what technologies can be developed' (322), but setting such limits is not really much of a problem since 'In a way we do this already because we can't afford to develop all technologies. Some are favoured and some are not. Or constraints may have to be levied by the community of nations on madmen or autarchs and fanaticism.' This touching trust in the community of nations and its wisdom (and in the sort of severe economic limitations – technological triage – that Jodie Foster encounters) rescues him from probing his dreams of escape into space. But of course it should not be thought of as escape. There are plenty of practical reasons, he thinks, for the project (in addition to the intellectual and aesthetic and, perhaps, the theological ones): we need to think about 'safeguarding the Earth from otherwise inevitable catastrophic impacts and hedging our bets on many other threats, known and unknown, to the environment' (he means, in addition to the threats we ourselves pose to it). 'If our long term survival is at stake, we have the responsibility to venture into other worlds' (377). Once we do, 'once we can send our machines and ourselves far from home, far from the planet – once we really enter *the theatre of the Universe* [italics mine] – we'll see strange stuff'. But not probably the strangest stuff:

It will not be we who reach Alpha Centauri and other nearby stars. It will be a species very like us, but with more of our strengths and less of our weakness, a species returned to circumstances far more like those for which it was originally evolved, more confident, far-seeing, capable and prudent – the sort of beings we would want to represent us in a Universe that, for all we know, is filled with species much older, much more powerful, and very different .... The vast differences that separate the stars are providential. The quarantine is lifted only for those with sufficient self-knowledge and judgment to have safely travelled from star to star. (398)

The doubts return. We cannot be trusted, not enough, after all. We are not the right stuff, yet. We need to evolve. We – or our most distant progeny – can become fit for the eternal and providential Universe (= God?) but only if we seize the moment and begin the task of transformation in earnest (so, get those 'early Martian pioneers, government sent and technologically expert' (336) right up there where they belong):

I believe it is healthy – indeed essential – to keep our frailty and fallibility firmly in mind. I worry about people who aspire to be 'god-like'. But as for a long term goal and a *sacred project*, there is one before us. On it the very survival of our species depends. If we have been locked and bolted into *a prison of the self*, here is *an escape hatch* – something worthy, something vastly larger than ourselves, a crucial act on behalf of humanity. Peopling other worlds unifies nations and ethnic groups, binds generations, and requires us to be both smart and wise. It liberates our nature and, in part, returns us to our beginnings. Even now this *new* telos is within our grasp. (404) (The last italics are his; the earlier are mine.)

The new telos is survival of the species, but it is also, apparently, liberation from worthlessness and an escape from ugly individuality; and it is a way of solving, out there, the dissensions and conflicts that have made the political and economic and religious history of this planet a long bloodbath in an endless bad dream (out there, we'll all learn 'just to get along'). So, a new telos, and one that renders irrelevant any questions about which technologies to pursue and which to junk (only those that will promote the survival of our evolving progeny *out there* need apply). Sagan does not tell us what the old telos was (was it also the survival of the species, so that the new is the old renewed?). What this means, in practical terms, from the perspective of the calculus of pleasure, is that one need no longer argue about whether, for instance, vaccinations and food for poor children are more important, more worthy of our time and money, than, for instance, breast and penis implants – not to mention the problem of biotech companies with their gene-altered foods, or – to be more specific – the US government's approval of 'the recombinant bovine growth hormone' that has found its way into American milk cows (see Daniel Bellow, 'Vermont, the Pure Food State', *The Nation*, 8 March 1999, 18-21). One can ignore global warming and ozone depletion and deforestation and pestilence and starvation and over-population and massive world poverty (all of these 'threats' made possible by technoscientific interventions that technical experts failed to abort) because technical experts are going to Mars to terraform it.

For all I know, Sagan's estimation of our future may be close to the mark. Maybe we've spoiled our home past saving it, maybe we'll have better luck next time, out there. I'm less interested here, however, in his predictions than I am in the pattern of values (and the anxieties beneath them) that shape his vision of who we are and what science is for. He well knows the perils and the complexities that attend on technological choices (elsewhere he is eloquent about them), but he can barely bring himself to admit them here (and in *Contact* the raptures of mystic optimism conceal them utterly). Instead, he uses religious and aesthetic images to camouflage what he cannot reveal, to himself, to his readers.

If science has been complicit (much too often) with bad corporate executives and worse (if possible) politicians, if the world is ruined, maybe science will find a way (that's what technocrats, in business and in government, always assure us of when the latest unconcealable disaster becomes news), maybe it will find a way for us, away from here, way out there. That rescue will be God's work, it will redeem science from any blame. It will also make it unnecessary to worry about reordering our priorities, here and now, from top to bottom.

Our real problem is: as a species, today, our morals are almost as archaic as our genetic makeup. That's why we have to escape, through the escape-into-space-hatch, into vast and loving spacetimes where evolution can make us what we were meant to be. A new telos for a new age! Newer bigger pies in newer bigger skies! Imagine Ellie (Sagan), on your TV screen, in a Lucretian pose. S/he is seized by divine pleasure and shuddering and gazes raptly into the bright infinitude of stars, intoning Sagan's accidental trademark (Sagan 1997, 3-10; Davidson 331, 342), 'Billions, billions, billions.' I wish we could hear Lucretius on that topic.

Leo Szilard meets historical amnesia
(or: Ronald Reagan meets Star Wars)

So much for the seductions of technomysticism. What happens when we look at the scientific project itself from a Lucretian perspective? Good scientists (let's call them that), who *do* try to pay attention to something like Lucretius' calculus of pleasure and are concerned to cause as little pain as possible and to reduce the quality and quantity of pain in the world, are not usually hard to spot. They tend to complain about shoddy notions and shoddy merchandise whether they are involved in their production or not. Their persistent motto is *Caveat Emptor* (let the consumer think twice). Their opposite numbers, the ordinary technoscientists, are also pretty easy to identify. They tend to insist, even when confronted with strong evidence to the contrary, that the products they make from scientific truths are intended primarily to benefit humankind and that the enrichment of their employers is distinctly less on their minds than the common, international good (for a useful description of this phenomenon, see Loewen 249-65). Presented with evidence that their products have turned out to be harmful, they will pretend to refute it and publicise their refutations with the help of the mechanisms of advertising. The good scientists, even when they band together (e.g. The Union of Concerned Scientists; The Federation of American Scientists; Physicians for Responsibility), don't get much help from those mechanisms. Why that should be the case we'll examine presently. But before we do that, I want to have a look at the myth of the Mad Scientist and what it is designed to hide from (and in) our collective (un)consciousness.

The movie has long since replaced the book – and not in Western Culture alone – as the chief instrument in the construction of our

142

collective (un)consciousness. It turns ideology into entertainment and entertainment back into ideology, instantly, transparently, unambiguously (it is not easy to argue, *pace* cult-studs, with what the eye has been persuaded it has seen, and when what it sees moves and tells a story, that story is, so to speak, an eye-witness account). For my immediate purposes, I'm interested only in what such stories and the myths they incarnate render invisible.

American Westerns, for instance, methodically make us *not* see what actually happened to 'American Indians ... the most lied-about subset of our population,' (Loewen 91). Another classic American genre, that of the Gangster (and its most durable sub-genre, Mafia-movie, just transformed by *The Sopranos* into super-art), is, on its surface, mostly concerned to assure us that Law and Order are invariably available to decent middle-class citizens, who, though sometimes incommoded and sometimes even hassled by the police, are ultimately served, and saved, by the police and the courts. (I pass over the genre's other great sub-genre, film noir, which is less interested in reassuring us than in arousing our anxieties about myths of law and order and about our own barely suppressed hankerings to walk on the wild side in those dark, mean streets.) For all the Mafia movie's reassurances about our system's health, its real message is about what we don't see, what we don't have the time or the nerve to think about, what we dare not learn anything about: corporate crime and white-collar crime. These crimes, it turns out, are so complicated, so filled with legalisms and complex arithmetic, that even journalists shy away from reporting on them (as did the American Press when the American public needed to know something about the Savings and Loans Scandals). What baffles journalists seldom attracts movie makers because these 'clean' crimes are mimetically intractable: it's hard to make boring, rich, white crooks dramatic and filmable whereas it's easy to watch various races and ethnicities gun each other down.

The Mafia movie says two things at the same time: these are the real dangers to our society and the police can deal with them (and they're funny and colourful in the bargain, these monsters); since these are the real dangers to society, don't worry if you now and then chance to read in the paper about some executive who's going to jail for fraud or some corporation that's being forced to pay a big (but not too big) fine because of some kind of dirty dealing. Think of John

143

Wayne (if your kid comes home from school asking what it was that happened on the Trail of Tears), think of Al Pacino (if your kid comes asking you why the old lady on the TV is crying because she lost her pension). In the former genre, Native Americans are effaced, in the latter, Big Business Crooks. (Some of these crooks, it's true, have begun to figure recently as villains in Thriller movies, but they or at least their henchmen are expert in the martial arts, and they are therefore very much at home in photogenic mayhem; they began arriving as Reaganomics got into high gear, but whether they will actually take possession of a genre of their own remains to be seen).

On its face, the myth of the Mad Scientist would appear to be mainly the work of frantic Luddites, designed by them to offer a throat-grabbing and unforgettable icon of all they feared and hated about of the dangers of modern technology, an image that fastens the blame for its evils, present, past and to come, directly on those directly responsible for them. But at the level of its invisible structure and in its most typical artistic incarnations, the myth does not so much warn us as reassure us. The mad scientist is, yes, mad, and yes, he threatens us, but just before The End flashes on the screen his minions are destroyed, along with his fiendish laboratory and his satanic experiments, and he, last of all, screams hysterically (triumphant or in despair, the convention is loose here) as he explodes and plunges into hell. It turns out that he was not as fatal as he fancied he was, the crazy physicist or mad biologist or nutcase chemist. Sometimes it is another (good) scientist who foils him, sometimes it's just the guy down the block.

Whoever does it, however they defeat him, what the tale and its myth tell us is this: There may be some bad apples in the Science Barrel (probably are), but science *does* work, and science *will* find a way. The mad scientist and his myth make it hard to tell a scientist with moral concerns from one without them. This (comforting) cartoon of what (some) (rotten) scientists do and want deflects our attention from the problem of distinguishing responsible from irresponsible science; it makes the moral scientist and the amoral scientist – since neither is mad – look similar if not identical.

You can make revisionist movies about Native Americans, can reverse that bad tradition, can show what they really suffered, how they were systematically cheated and murdered and maligned. Hav-

144

ing done that you can, having turned the genre inside out and on its head, you can help it die out. But it's hard to make pictures of invisible crime: stockbrokers and corporate executives pilfering from each other or from their clients or from people they've never seen whose lives they destroy; or technoscientists in their labs, cooking the evidence, losing the experiment, signing on with the pharmaceutical company or the biotech conglomerate just at the moment when their pure, theoretical knowledge is most crucial to corporations that need such knowledge in order to sustain their progess: that is, the 'improvement' of their product and the growth of their profits. (For those interested in such things, there is what seems to be a relevant story in the *New York Times*, 16 August 1999, A10, 'Scientist's Shift to Industry Puts a Report in Question'.) If we think of what the myth of the Mad Scientist tries to hide from us, we can begin to think about how to distinguish not the mad, but the bad scientist, from the good one. And we can then begin to think of what it must be like, for the good ones, to be so powerful – and so helpless.

Leo Szilard is not a household or media name. Although he has recently been the subject of William Lanouette's exemplary biography and was honoured, in 1998, by centenary celebrations in both his native Hungary and in the US (sponsored by the American Physical Society), he remains, in the words of Lanouette (xix) 'largely a forgotten man, a genius in the shadows of the world he helped create'. He turns up regularly in the older histories of the Bomb, often in sympathetic focus, but for the most part, despite the biography and the centenaries, he seems now to be drifting into shorter sentences and briefer footnotes, that is to say, into historical oblivion, the last place he belongs. Cinematically speaking, a sure index to his neglect is the manner in which he is all but effaced from an ambitious Hollywood movie about the making of the Bomb, *Fat Man and Little Boy* (1989); more telling still, he is totally absent from an otherwise acute analysis of the film's historical inaccuracies (Carnes 246-9; the entire story of the Bomb, however, is brilliantly represented by Roger Spottiswood's three-hour film, *Hiroshima*, 1995, a Canadian-Japanese production).

But it is Sagan who makes Szilard disappear most effectively. In the course of his meditations on 'the power of the exponential', Sagan suddenly thinks of a flawless example of his topic (1997, 198-9): 'Nuclear fission was first thought of in London in September 1933 by an emigré Hungarian physicist named Leo Szilard.' Sagan then proceeds to give a lucid description of the flowering of Szilard's idea. This completed, he follows Szilard from England to the United States and his early work there in atomic physics. He then mentions that 'Szilard convinced Albert Einstein to write his famous letter to President Roosevelt urging the United States to build an atomic bomb. Szilard played a major role in the uranium chain reaction in Chicago in 1942, which in fact led to the atomic bomb. He spent the rest of his life warning about the dangers he had been the first to conceive. He had found, in yet another way, the awesome power of the exponential.'

Sagan is interested, naturally, in the tragic irony that arises from Szilard's encounter with the force of exponentiality and his hopeless efforts to undo what he had begun. But in the process, he manages to depoliticise and dehistoricise Szilard's struggles and thus to deprive them of their essential meaning. Sagan ignores the fact that Szilard was Jewish and that he had fled Nazi Germany (emigré?). It was his fear that the Nazis might develop nuclear weapons that prompted him to get Einstein to write that letter to Roosevelt. Furthermore, though Sagan acknowledges that Szilard spent 'the rest of his life warning about the dangers of the weapon', he fails to mention that Szilard's passionate protests had begun before the war was over and before the bombs had been dropped on Japan. It is his early, bitter conflicts with politics in general and with the military in particular that are at the heart of his story. Sagan was no stranger to such conflicts (he allegorises them with some acrimony in *Contact*), but he has hidden them here, not only because he wants to emphasise the terrible beauty of the exponential but also because this story, this whole story, is one that he and many of his fellow scientists seem disinclined to ponder: it reminds them of their dependence for their livelihoods and their laboratories on the military-industrial complex (which includes the United States Legislature), and it reminds them, too, that in any real argument they may have with the miliary-industrial complex, it isn't the complex that's likely to lose (Garwin 224-7).

For my immediate purposes, Szilard's story is less important for what it implies about Truman's decision to bomb Hiroshima and Nagasaki than for what it reveals about the peculiar dynamic that fuels the story behind that story, about the nature and structure of scientific involvement outside the academy, 'in the real world', about the ambiguities that confront the moral imagination (and sometimes petrify it) when that dynamic takes over. I happen to think that Truman and his advisors did something evil when they dropped those bombs, but the ferocious collision of perspectives that marked the Smithsonian Museum's 'Enola Gay' Exhibition in 1995 should remind us that this debate will never really end. What I want to focus on here is the figure of Szilard, to see what clues it might provide to the question of what it means for a scientist *qua* scientist to make choices. I want to see what Szilard still has to tell us about the meaning of a moment when a scientific truth becomes a techno-logical product.

From 1941, when preparations for the creation of the Bomb began in earnest, until the spring of 1945, when it was almost ready to be dropped, Szilard had dutifully performed his share of the work of making the Bomb by co-designing 'with Fermi the world's first nuclear reactor' (Lanouette xvi, 223; Rhodes 508). But in March 1945, just four months before the Bomb had its spectacularly successful debut at Trinity, Arizona, Szilard asked Einstein for a letter to accompany one that he had written to the President. In his letter, Einstein wrote: 'I understand he [Szilard] now is greatly concerned about the lack of adequate contact between scientists who are doing this work and those members of your Cabinet who are responsible for formulating policy.'

What Szilard is greatly concerned about, in fact, is his growing sense that the use of the Bomb against the Japanese, whatever purpose that use might be felt to have, would be immoral; he is no less concerned about his complete realisation that Vannever Bush, General Leslie Groves, and James B. Conant would have nothing but contempt for what must appear to them as the cheap quibbles and craven qualms of scientists who opposed them (Szilard 181). Bush and Conant were members of the newly created National Defense Research Coun-cil. Bush, who was the Council's chairman, was an electrical engineer as well as being President of the Carnegie Institute. Conant was a professor of Chemistry who had become President of Harvard (McKay 63). General Groves, the person in charge of the construction of the Pentagon (a dazzling irony), had been put in charge of the Manhattan Project, and it is generally agreed that he was pretty much the reason the Bomb was finished 'on time' (McKay 69). Szilard, frustrated, unable to approach Roosevelt through the chain of command (the

Council) decides to write to the President directly (with Einstein and the President's wife smoothing his way). And all that seems to be going well, but – the President dies before getting the letter (Szilard 181-2; Lanouette 259-63).

Hoping to address the new President, Truman, Szilard drafted 'A Petition to The President of the United States' (17 July 1945: Szilard 211-12) which he circulated at his Met Lab. He got fifty-three signatures, including most of the leading physicists and many of the leading biologists. 'The signatures of the chemists were conspicuously absent. This was so striking that I went over to the chemistry department to discover what the trouble was. What I discovered was rather disturbing: the chemists argued that what we must determine was solely whether more lives would be saved by using the bomb or by continuing the war without using the bomb.' Some people said they would sign if the wording of the petition became milder, and a second draft 'drew a somewhat larger number of signatures – but not a significantly larger number' (Szilard 187). The signatories asked that 'the United States shall not resort to the use of atomic bombs in this war unless the terms which will be imposed upon Japan have been made public in detail and Japan knowing these terms has refused to surrender; that in such an event the question of whether or not to use atomic bombs be decided by you in the light of the considerations presented in this petition as well as all the other moral responsibilities which are involved'. The considerations, in the main body of the petition, point out the unimaginable precedent a use of the bomb will set, they sketch the kinds of arms races that the new world will be seeing, they invoke the moral imperative that the possession of such a weapon lays upon its possessor. It is a stern, temperate, chilling document. Children in American schools should read it along with the Declaration of Independence and the Bill of Rights. (The rest of us should read it, again, or for the first time, and keep on reading it.)

Szilard, though worried about how to get the petition to the new President, was forced to send it through regular channels, which meant through General Groves, who was to hand it over to President Truman in Postdam (its delivery would be strangely delayed). Once the petition was sealed and apparently on its way, Szilard reflected on what he had just tried to do:

148

> I knew the bomb would be dropped, that we had lost the fight.
> And when it was actually dropped my overall feeling was a
> feeling of relief. A component of this relief is that we were
> completely bottled up in our discussions – it was not possible to
> get real issues before the public because of secrecy. Suddenly the
> secrecy was dropped and it was possible to tell people what this
> was about and what we were facing in this country. (Szilard 188)

Not quite. After the bombs have been dropped, Szilard announces his
intention to declassify the petition. After some delay in getting permission to do so, he learns that General Groves has reclassified the
petition 'Secret'. From reliable sources he gathers that what is now
secret about the document is that it might lead its readers to 'conclude
that there must have been some dissension in the project prior to the
termination of the war, which might have slowed down the work of the
project which was conducted under the Army' (Szilard 188).

Szilard never quite got a fix on Groves or Bush or Conant. He did
not guess that it was not exactly Truman or even Roosevelt before him
who was really calling the shots (General Groves, on Truman's taking
responsibility for dropping the bomb: 'Truman did not so much say
"yes" as not say "no". It would have taken a lot of nerve to say "no" at
that time', Jungk 208). It's likely that as soon as General Groves was
at the wheel, the fates of Hiroshima and Nagasaki were sealed. When
military scientists in Europe had ascertained (November 1944) that
the Germans did not in fact have the atom bomb, one of them en-
thused: 'Isn't it wonderful that the Germans have no atom bomb? Now
we won't have to have to use ours.' To which one of his colleagues
replied: 'You don't know Groves. If we have such a bomb, then we'll use
it' (McKay 111). Nothing strange there. For many people, vocations are
identities, destinies. I was a Latin teacher, and I would have found
myself very frustrated had I not had the luck to earn a living by
teaching the language I love. Actors have to get themselves up on that
stage. Chefs have to get themselves into that kitchen. Scientists have
to complete that experiment and falsify that theory. And generals and
the bombmakers who work for them have to employ their death
gadgets, they have to drop that bomb.

The problem with Szilard's verisimilar version of the bomb's narrative, the reason that the dominant ideologies dislike and fear it, is that

it puts General Groves and his team squarely in the centre of the action and reduces Oppenheimer and his fellow scientists, able though they are in the performance of their necessary functions, to important and distinguished employees. (For Groves' attitude to his scientific help, see Groueff 8, 32-4, Rhodes 504-11; for his hatred of Szilard, see Lanouette 269, 305-13). In versions of the bombbuilding story that accept the official version (Truman's, Groves'), while an irritating Szilard wrings his hands in the wings and while General Groves hovers discreetly (but ubiquitously) in the background, Oppenheimer and his scientists and Truman and his team of professionals form the tale's complex, harmonious core. For the idea of rational atomic research to work, for scientific cultures to continue flourishing after Hiroshima, they need a narrative about how wise scientists and wise politicians (and wise business leaders) once, in a crucial hour, came together, and, with the help of military men and with implied public consent (in wartime the public could not exactly be informed), wisely provided their nation with the atomic defensive weapon that it (almost) could not have done without.

Most of us now recognise (if only unconsciously) that this narrative is sentimental (and cynical) drivel because we have learned that Szilard was mistaken in supposing it was 'possible to tell people what this was about and what we are facing in this century'. But if we know that the dominant ideology's master narrative is unreal, if we know that this is the narrative that General Groves and Bush and Conant and Truman and their successors constructed for us to believe in, we also know that it is *the* master narrative about how the marriage of science and technology is supposed to function in a democratic technological society. And we also know that this is the narrative that journalists, for instance, keep writing and rewriting, against their instincts and their observations and their consciences, after listening to the information supplied them by a Pentagon spokesman or by a lobbyist for the weapons industry or by a congressman who wants some jobs in the weapons industry located in his district or by a President who wants to secure his place in history.

Szilard, of course, didn't call it quits. He kept trying to get the message out, he kept trying to wake the conscience of his new nation and the consciences of his peers. He kept running into decent people with decent intentions. He kept finding good scientists and even good

150

politicians (Lanouette 356-76, 404-64; cf. Rhodes 754). But the machine they all lived and worked in was too intricate and too exact for them to counter it successfully. Groves built it and Groves knew how to operate it in ways Szilard and the helpers he encountered could never begin to fathom. (For his final struggle with Groves and its luckless aftermath, see Jungk 221-59 and Lanouette 281-301.) Szilard had realised this (almost) by the time he came to write: 'I have been asked whether I would agree that the tragedy of the scientist is that he is able to bring about great advances in our knowledge, which mankind may then proceed to use for purposes of destruction. My answer is that this is not the tragedy of the scientist; it is the tragedy of mankind' (Szilard 229). Even so, he kept on trying to challenge the world to try to find ways out of its tragedy until he died in California in 1964.

Lewis Wolpert, whose version of the Szilard story is rather different from mine (not to mention Lanouette's), uses these words of Oppenheimer's to point toward the moral he gives his tale:

> The scientist is not responsible for the laws of nature, but it is the scientist's job to find out how these laws operate. It is the scientist's job to find the ways in which these laws can serve the human will. However, it is not the scientist's job to determine whether a hydrogen bomb should be used. That responsibility rests with the American people and their chosen representatives. (156)

To bomb or not to bomb, that 'was a political decision and not a scientific decision', says Wolpert, echoing Oppenheimer (for Oppenheimer's own use of his 'scientific prestige to influence political decisions', see Lanouette 270, 292-3 and Herken 21, 24). So Szilard's tale shows that he was at best quixotic in his belief that scientists should have some share in suggesting what should become of their ideas. From this perspective, Szilard was not wrong when he nudged Einstein to nudge Roosevelt into building the bomb, but he was clearly in the wrong when he tried to interfere with the labours of Groves and Bush and Conant. And – well, he was finally right because 'one of the most important obligations to emerge from this tale is that of openness, exemplified by his [Szilard's] emphasis after the war on telling the public about the implications of scientific knowledge .... The necessity for the public to be informed about science and its implications is a major obligation for scientists' (Wolpert 157-8).

In the two decades after Hiroshima, Szilard did try to educate the public, and not the least part of that attempt to educate was (and is) his own story, which shows how telling people what the Bomb is all about 'and what we are facing in this country', is a lot harder, as Oppenheimer certainly knew, than his (and Wolpert's) bland pieties about the citizens and their chosen representatives and the responsibilities that they share would suggest. (For a recent reminder of how hard 'telling what it's all about' is, see the obituary in the *New York Times*, 31 July 1999, 'G.C. Minor; 62, an Engineer Who Criticized Nuclear Power'.)

One is sometimes tempted to think that the only hope for good scientists, such as the Union of Concerned Scientists, is to imitate the corporate executives of the 1930s. The objects of unequivocal hatred during the depth of Depression, those shrewd gentlemen hired themselves squadrons of publicity firms to reconstruct and beautify their images. After their contributions in World War II and the efforts of their admen, they became and remained, in the following decades, fixed in the American collective (un)consciousness as objects of admiration. The good scientists, of course, are not hated, they are merely mostly unknown; they have got to find some way of making it impossible for the media to ignore them (except when it's time to push the Doomsday's Clock closer to Nada, a brief but vivid sound-bite) and of getting their many messages out. In this electronic, Baudrillardique and funhouse world probably only Public Relations can win the day. Perhaps there is also some hope here from the Internet, where I happened to find (looking for Leo Szilard) the announcement of the Leo Szilard Lectureship Award, established in 1974 by the Forum on Physics and Society. Its purpose is 'to recognise outstanding accomplishments by physicists in promoting the use of physics for the benefit of society in such areas as the environment, arms control, and science policy. The lecture format is intended to increase the visibility of those who have promoted the use of physics for the benefit of society.' You increase visibility by getting public relations firms to do it for you.

Back to Szilard, whose tale transforms the Faust-genre utterly. Scientists, politicians, businessmen and military men are crammed together into a small space and a desperate time, and the fate of nations and maybe of the world is in their hands. They must learn to work together, under impossible conditions, in order to produce something astonishing and terrifying. In various versions of this founding tale (some by eyewitnesses, some by historians) we find frequent mention of teamwork. And they did, those hard-pressed, baffled, heroic people, they did succeed in a joint enterprise whose success continues to seem all but miraculous. They succeeded because they had come upon the right pattern for their desperate enterprise, the one provided by, and best symbolized by, General Groves. That pattern more nearly suits military oligarchy than it does a democratic republic. It has, for good reasons and for bad, enormous need of secrecy. It does not want its citizens or even most of their representatives to know what it's doing and it's not much interested – here Oppenheimer and Wolpert are right – in what scientists think or feel about what is being done with scientific truths. Scientists are precious, yes, they are essential, they are priceless, but, when the chips are down, they are only workers, they are only special people paid to do a special job. Their intellectual virtues, their moral judgments, have no more importance in the 'real world' that the general and his technocrats manipulate as they choose than would those of a poet or a parson or a teacher of ethics. They are wizards in bondage.

It is in part because the Szilard story is either forgotten (he finds no mention in the informative essays on nuclear warfare and nuclear control by Sidney Drell, past President of the American Physics Society) or misread that Edward Teller found such smooth access to Ronald Reagan. It's true that Reagan had a richly developed taste for apocalyptic iconography, that he was ever anxious to get his hands on the controls of the latest in shiny military hardware – that he was, in short, an easy mark. But mostly by the time that Teller began selling Reagan on Star Wars, America's citizens had begun to understand, if only in their collective (un)consciousness, that they were not being told everything (or much of anything useful) about the incalculable defense budget and what it bought. They began to be aware, also, that the weapons industry is what matters to the American economy, they were figuring out that lobbyists for this and related industries had more hope of impressing and influencing their elected representatives than they could ever hope to have. Nuclear Control, moreover, had long since become Baroque Theatre (and Reagan was superbly gifted at performing in it and at being photographed performing in it). The amount of time in national discourse (for instance, in the media) devoted to the presentation of scientific truth to the public, never excessive, dwindled further, steadily, in the years when Teller was telling Reagan about the magic shield he had devised for our salvation. The wizard, briefly let off his leash, imagined himself set free.

Conclusion

What would be Lucretius' perspective on Szilard's story? If he was disheartened to see space-scientists and cosmologists inventing new mystery religions, I think he would be appalled to see the masters of atomic truth unable, and in some cases unwilling, to provide the knowledge they had which alone would allow the people to make sensible judgments about *true pleasures*. He would certainly not like seeing Memmius (who bears some resemblance to General Groves) controlling the game, determining the calculus of pleasure. The tricky Oppenheimer/Wolpert distinction between a scientific decision and a political decision blurs the true and relevant distinction that Szilard's story shows must be made when we (the citizens, our representatives, the scientists and politicians and generals who work for us) try to decide whether a new technological product is going to minimise our suffering or increase it, perhaps exponentially. (*Our suffering*: could be our nation's, could be our species', could be our planet's and all that it contains.) Political decisions about technological products that are promulgated in the language of tribal religions and their value systems (our nation, our God, our blood = morality) and that are made without benefit of accurate and *honest* scientific estimates of their 'long-term' effects on us and on our world are invalid, immoral, and, eventually, ruinous. That's how Lucretius would rate them on his *vera voluptas* meter. Bad scientists (not mad, not amoral), bad scientists who work for bad technocrats and produce absurd or fatal luxuries instead of needful things and creature comforts do poorly when Lucretius measures them against the demands of true pleasure. There is no need to apply this measure to bad scientists who work for worse technocrats to produce things that bring unnecessary pain to humankind and unnecessary damage to the planet it inhabits. Their definitions of 'necessary', usually crafted with the same rhetoric that Groves and Truman and Oppenheimer and Conant and Bush devised to sell their product, don't persuade Lucretius.

Bad scientists already have plenty of PR men. I hope those good scientists somehow manage to get hold of some good PR men of their own. What bothers me almost as much as the problems good scientists have with advertising truth is that the heirs of General Groves often have some say in making up reading lists in high schools, junior colleges, and even colleges. How are aspiring scientists and aspiring citizens to get the knowledge of true pleasure that they need in order to make sure that their technological choices are scientifically *and* morally sound, that they are merely political as seldom as possible? How would they develop that habit of mind?

I've retired from the education racket, and making up syllabi is the last thing on my mind. But I can still scribble out a reading list for a Text Course called 'True Pleasure', a course in which an unstable and effective mixture of science and non-science majors would read together and would argue about the following books: *The Voyage of the Beagle* by Charles Darwin, *The Blind Watchmaker* by Richard Dawkins, John Hersey's *Hiroshima* (1946) and relevant pages from Hershberg's life of James Conant (291-304) where his efforts to defuse the impact of Hersey's book are carefully documented, *Early Greek Philosophy* by Jonathan Barnes, *Genesis* (few young people who read it in its entirety will be likely to prefer it, as science, to Darwin, but in case they do, a few chapters of Daniel Dennett's *Darwin's Dangerous Idea* might help them), P.N. Singer's translation of Galen's *Selected Works* (Oxford World's Classics), Jules Verne's terrifying masterpiece, *Paris in the Twentieth Century*, Zamyatin's *We*, H.G. Wells' *When the Sleeper Wakes*, J.G. Ballard's *Concrete Island*, Leo Szilard's *His Version of the Facts*, and Lucretius' *On the Nature of Things*.

Then they might all go off together to see a really great movie, Michael Mann's *The Insider*, which is not so much about corporate executives who lie to the public and media moguls who help them do it as it is about scientists who find the courage to stop lying.

Bibliography

Ament, Ernest J. 'The *Anti-Lucretius* of Cardinal Polignac', *Transactions of the American Philological Society* 101 (1970) 29-49.

Amory, Anne. *'Obscura de re lucida carmina*: Science and Poetry in *De Rerum Natura*', *Yale Classical Review* 21 (1969) 145-68.

Aldridge, A. Owen. *Voltaire and the Century of Light*. (Princeton 1975).

Asmis, Elizabeth. 'Lucretius' Venus and Stoic Zeus', *Hermes* 110 (1982) 459-70.

Austin, Norman. 'Translation as Baptism: Dryden's Lucretius', *Arion* (Winter 1968) 576-602.

Bollack, Mayotte. *La raison de Lucrèce* (Paris 1978).

Bradley, Edward. 'Lucretius the Melancholy', *Classical Journal* 67 (1972) 317-22.

Bright, John. 'The Plague and the Structure of the *DRN*', *Latomus* 30 (1971) 607-32.

Campbell, Joan. 'Science and Religion', in Terzian and Bilson, 254-60.

Carnes, Mark C. *Past Imperfect: History According to the Movies*. (New York 1995).

Chatterjee, Kalika Ranjan. *Studies in Tennyson as a Poet of Science*. (New Delhi 1974).

Clay, Diskin. *Lucretius and Epicurus*. (Ithaca, New York 1983).

Colley, Ann C. *Tennyson and Madness*. (Athens, Georgia 1983).

Commager, H.S., Jr. 'Lucretius' Interpretation of the Plague', *Harvard Studies in Classical Philology* 62 (1957) 105-18.

Costa, C.D.N. *De Rerum Natura Liber V*. (Oxford 1984).

Dalzell, Alexander. 'Lucretius', *Cambridge History of Classical Literature*, vol. 2: *Latin Literature*. (Cambridge 1982) 207-29.

———— *The Criticism of Didactic Poetry: Essays on Lucretius, Virgil and Ovid*. (Toronto 1998).

Davidson, Keay. *Carl Sagan: A Life*. (New York 1999).

Dawkins, Richard. *The Blind Watchmaker: Why the Evidence of Evolution Reveals a Universe Without Design*. (New York 1986).

Dennett, Daniel C. *Darwin's Dangerous Idea: Evolution and the Meanings of Life*. (New York 1995).

Dodds, E.R. *The Ancient Concept of Progress*. (Oxford 1973).

157

Bibliography

Drell, Sidney D. *In the Shadow of the Bomb: Physics and Arms Control.* (American Physics Institute: New York 1993).

Fleischmann, Wolfgang Bernard. 'The Debt of the Enlightenment to Lucretius', *Studies in Voltaire and the Eighteenth Century* 29 (1963) 631-43.

——— *Lucretius and English Literature, 1680-1740.* (Paris 1964).

Fowler, Peta. 'Lucretian Conclusions', *Classical Closures*, ed. D. Roberts, F. Dunn, Don Fowler. (Princeton 1997) 112-38.

Fusil, C.-A. 'Lucrèce et les philosophes du XVIIIe Siècle', *Revue d'Histoire Littéraire de la France* 35 (1928) 161-76.

Gale, Monica. *Myth and Poetry in Lucretius.* (Cambridge 1994).

Garwin, Richard L. 'The Relationship of Science and Power', in Terzian and Bilson, 221-7.

Godwin, John. *De Rerum Natura IV* (Warminster 1986).

——— *De Rerum Natura VI* (Warminster 1991).

Greene, Brian. *The Elegant Universe: Superstrings, Hidden Dimensions, and the Quest for the Ultimate Theory.* (New York 1999).

Groueff, Stephane. *Manhattan Project: The Untold Story of the Making of the Atomic Bomb.* (Boston 1967).

Hadzsits, Walter. *Lucretius and his Influence.* (New York 1935).

Herken, Gregg. *Cardinal Choices: Presidential Science Advising from the Atomic Bomb to SDI.* (Oxford 1992).

Hersey, John. *Hiroshima.* (New York 1946).

Hershberg, James G. *James B. Conant: Harvard to Hiroshima and the Making of the Nuclear Age.* (New York 1993).

Hutchinson, Lucy. *De Rerum Natura*, ed. Hugh de Quehen (London and Ann Arbor 1996).

Jenkyns, Richard. *Virgil's Experience: Nature and History: Times, Names, Places.* (Oxford 1999).

Jones, Howard. *The Epicurean Tradition.* (London 1989).

Joy, Lynn Sumida. *Gassendi the Atomist: Advocate of History in an Age of Science.* (Cambridge 1987).

Jungk, Robert. *Brighter Than a Thousand Suns*, tr. James Cleugh. (New York 1958).

Kenney, E.J. 'The Medium and the Message'. Review of P.H. Schrijvers' *Horror ac Divina Voluptas. Classical Review* 28 (1978) 348-51.

Kinsey, T.E. 'The Melancholy of Lucretius', *Arion* 3 (1964) 115-30.

Lamont, Lansing. *Day of Trinity.* (New York 1965).

Lanouette, William (with Bela Silard). *Genius in the Shadows: A Biography of Leo Szilard.* (Toronto 1993; Chicago 1994).

Loewen, James W. *Lies My Teacher Told Me.* (New York 1995).

McGinn, Colin. *The Mysterious Flame: Conscious Minds in a Material World.* (New York 1999).

McKay, Alwyn. *The Making of the Atomic Age.* (Oxford 1984)

Martha, Constant. *Poème de Lucrèce: Morale – Religion – Science* (Paris 1896: 5th ed.).

Mason, John Hope. *The Irresistible Diderot*. (London 1982).

Minyard, J.D. *Lucretius and the Late Republic: An Esssay in Roman Intellectual History. Mnemosyne Supplement* 90. (Leiden 1985).

Mitsis, Philip. *Epicurus' Ethical Theory: The Pleasures of Invulnerability*. (Ithaca 1988).

Munro, H.A.J. *T. Lucreti Cari: De Rerum Natura, Libri Sex*. (Cambridge 1893; 4th ed. Finally Revised).

Patin, M. *Études sur la Poésie Latine*. (Paris 1914; 5th ed.).

Rhodes, Richard. *The Making of the Atomic Bomb*. (New York 1986).

Rudd, Niall. *The Classical Tradition in Operation*. (Toronto 1994).

Sagan, Carl. *Billions and Billions: Thoughts on Life and Death at Birth of the Millennium*. (New York 1997).

———— *Contact*. (New York 1985; paper: 1986).

———— *Pale Blue Dot: A Vision of the Human Future in Space*. (New York 1994).

Salem, Jean. *La mort n'est rien pour nous: Lucrèce et l'éthique*. (Paris 1990).

Santayana, George. *Three Philosophical Poets*. (Cambridge, Mass. 1910).

Saylor, Charles. 'Man, Animal, and the Bestial in Lucretius', *Classical Journal* 67 (1972) 306-16.

Schmid, Wolfgang. 'Lukrez und der Wandel seines Bild', *Antike und Abendland*. (1946) 193-219.

Sedley, David. *Lucretius and the Transformation of Greek Wisdom* (London 1998).

Segal, Charles. *Lucretius on Death and Anxiety*. (Princeton 1990).

Shaw, Marion. *Alfred Tennyson*. (Atlantic Highlands, N.J. 1988).

Smith, Ian H. 'Le rêve de d'Alembert and the DRN', *Journal of the Australasian Universities: Language and Literature Association* 10 (1959) 128-34.

Spink, J.S. *French Free-Thought from Gassendi to Voltaire*. (London 1960).

Stove, David. *The Plato Cult: And Other Philosophical Follies*. (Oxford, Blackwell 1991).

Szilard, Leo. *Leo Szilard: His Version of the Facts: Selected Recollections and Correspondence*, ed. Spencer R. Weart and Gertrude Weiis Szilard, vol. 2. (MIT Press 1978).

Terzian, Yervant and Elizabeth Bilson, eds, *Carl Sagan's Universe*. (Cambridge 1997).

Thompson, Silvanus P. *The Life of William Thomson, Baron Kelvin of Largs*, 2 vols. (London 1910).

Thorn, Michael. *Tennyson*. (London 1992).

Toohey, Peter. *Epic Lessons: An Introduction to Ancient Didactic Poetry* (London 1996).

Townend, G.B. 'The Fading of Memmius', *Classical Quarterly* 22 (1972) 267-83.

Turner, Frank M. 'Lucretius Among the Victorians', *Victorian Studies* 16 (1972-3) 329-48.

Tyndall, John. *Fragments of Science: A Series of Detached Essays, Addresses and Reviews*, 2 vols (London 1892).

Weinberg, Steven. *Dreams of a Final Theory: The Scientist's Search for the Ultimate Laws of Nature.* (New York 1992).

Wilson, Arthur M. *Diderot.* (Oxford 1972).

Winn, James Alexander. *John Dryden and his World.* (New Haven 1987).

Wolpert, Lewis. *The Unnatural Nature of Science.* (Cambridge, Mass. 1993).

Index

161

Index

voluptas atque horror, 5, 12, 15, 19, 47, 93, 96, 116, 118, 121-2, 142

war, 59-64, 69, 70, 146-54

wealth, 53-6, 69, 70
Wilson, Arthur M., 95
wives, 43-6, 50
Wolpert, Lewis, 151-2, 153

CPSIA information can be obtained at www.ICGtesting.com
Printed in the USA
LVOW01s0016290714

396466LV00004B/72/P

9 780715 628829